THE LIFE OF MERESAMUN

MW00378894

THE LIFE OF MERESAMUN

A TEMPLE SINGER IN ANCIENT EGYPT

edited by

EMILY TEETER *and* JANET H. JOHNSON

THE ORIENTAL INSTITUTE MUSEUM PUBLICATIONS · NUMBER 29
THE ORIENTAL INSTITUTE OF THE UNIVERSITY OF CHICAGO

Library of Congress Control Number: 2008942017
ISBN-10: 1-885923-60-0
ISBN-13: 978-1-885923-60-8

© 2009 by The University of Chicago. All rights reserved.
Published 2009. Printed in the United States of America.

The Oriental Institute, Chicago

This volume has been published in conjunction with the exhibition
The Life of Meresamun: A Temple Singer in Ancient Egypt, presented
at The Oriental Institute Museum, February 10–December 6, 2009.

Oriental Institute Museum Publications No. 29

The Series Editors Leslie Schramer and Thomas G. Urban would like to thank
Sabahat Adil and Kaye Oberhausen for their help in the production of this volume.

Published by The Oriental Institute of the University of Chicago
1155 East 58th Street
Chicago, Illinois 60637 USA
oi.uchicago.edu

Meresamun's name appears in hieroglyphs on the title page.

This publication has been made possible in part
by the generous support of Philips Healthcare.

Printed by M&G Graphics, Chicago, Illinois.

The paper used in this publication meets the minimum requirements of American National Standard for
Information Service – Permanence of Paper for Printed Library Materials, ANSI Z39.48-1984
∞

TABLE OF CONTENTS

Foreword. *Gil J. Stein* 7

Preface. *Geoff Emberling* 9

Contributors 11

Map of Egypt 12

Outline Chronology 13

Meresamun's Egypt. *Emily Teeter* (cat. no. 1) 15

Inside the Temple: The Role and Function of Temple Singers. *Emily Teeter* 25

    Ritual Music. *Emily Teeter* (cat. nos. 2–10) 30

    Ritual Objects. *Emily Teeter* (cat. nos. 11–14) 43

    Oracles. *Emily Teeter* (cat. nos. 15–16) 46

    Animal Cults and Animal Mummies. *Elise V. MacArthur* (cat. nos. 17–20) 49

Meresamun's Life Outside the Temple. *Emily Teeter* 55

    Home Furnishings (cat. nos. 21–47) 60

    Household Cults. *Emily Teeter* (cat. nos. 48–54) 71

    Fertility and Birth Rituals. *Elise V. MacArthur* (cat. nos. 55–61) 76

    Social, Economic, and Legal Rights of Women in Egypt. *Janet H. Johnson* (cat. nos. 62–64) 82

    Women and Their Employment. *Magaera Lorenz* (cat. nos. 65–72) 98

Radiological Report on the Mummy of Meresamun. *Michael Vannier, M.D.* 111

Glossary 119

Bibliography 121

Checklist of the Exhibit 127

Concordance of Oriental Institute Museum Registration Numbers 129

Index of Egyptian Names 131

General Index 133

FOREWORD

GIL J. STEIN
DIRECTOR, ORIENTAL INSTITUTE

One of the most compelling aspects of ancient studies is their power to reach across time and allow us to make a connection with the people of the Near East thousands of years in the past. When we see a child's toy, or read a scribal student's letter to his parents in which he complains about his teachers and classmates, we can bypass the differences of time, language, or culture and feel the frisson of recognition that these were people not all that different from ourselves — men, women, and children who played, studied (or didn't study), married, bore children, and experienced the joys and sorrows of everyday life. Recognizing the people of the ancient world as actual people, and not just as "Egyptians" or "Sumerians" has the effect of increasing our respect for the achievements of these civilizations, because we can understand at a deep level that the magnificent temples, palaces, and art masterpieces were the work of people who could just as easily have been our neighbors and friends. The Oriental Institute's special exhibit The Life of Meresamun: A Temple Singer in Ancient Egypt gives us a rare and spectacular opportunity to reach across time in this way.

Since the mummy of Meresamun was acquired by the Oriental Institute in 1920, the vibrant colors, beautiful paintings, and near-perfect preservation of the inner coffin enclosing her remains have entranced visitors to our Museum's Joseph and Mary Grimshaw Egyptian Gallery. However, the current exhibit allows us to experience Meresamun in an entirely new light. Thanks to the creativity and scholarship of our exhibit curator Emily Teeter, we can see Meresamun as an individual. By combining insights from archaeology, philology, ancient history, and modern medical technology it becomes possible to understand Meresamun as an individual — a woman from a prosperous family who lived and worked in a prestigious social and ritual role as a singer in the Interior of the Temple of Amun, the pre-eminent god of Thebes. Through generations of study of the architecture, inscriptions, and art at the Karnak and Luxor temples, we can more or less understand the turbulent political milieu of Thebes during the Third Intermediate Period, around 800 B.C., during Meresamun's lifetime. The carefully selected artifacts in this exhibit, drawn from the Institute's collections, show us the kinds of hair ornaments she might have worn, the vessels she would have used to eat and drink, and the style of mirror she might have used in her daily preparations before she went to perform her ritual service to Amun. We can see the funerary stelae and sculptures she might have passed on her way to and from the temple — perhaps pausing to remember a departed friend or family member. And thanks to the extraordinary CT scanning imagery developed by Philips Healthcare, we can gain unprecedented insights into Meresamun as a physical person who lived, had health problems, and eventually died. Dr. Michael Vannier's radiological expertise even allows us to generate computer reconstructions of her actual physical appearance. In short — against all odds of time and preservation — this exhibit allows us to see Meresamun as an actual individual. This is a remarkable achievement.

I want to thank Oriental Institute Museum Director Geoff Emberling for his efforts to plan, coordinate, and make this exhibit a reality. Emily Teeter has done a remarkable job with scholarly rigor and creativity as Curator in designing this extraordinary exhibit and in co-editing the catalog with Janet Johnson. We deeply appreciate the efforts of the University of Chicago Hospitals and of Dr. Michael Vannier in the CT radiological examination of Meresamun's mummy. Thomas Urban and Leslie Schramer of the Oriental Institute Publications Office have done a wonderful job in the design and production of the exhibit catalog. Finally, I want to acknowledge the Exelon Corporation, Philips Healthcare, and Rita and Kitty Picken for their generosity and the support that made this special exhibit possible.

PREFACE

GEOFF EMBERLING
MUSEUM DIRECTOR, ORIENTAL INSTITUTE

The Oriental Institute began a program of special exhibits in the Marshall and Doris Holleb Family Special Exhibits Gallery in winter 2006. These exhibits give us the chance to highlight Oriental Institute research, to display objects not otherwise on view, and to focus on themes that are not emphasized in our permanent galleries.

Each exhibit in our series, and each catalog, has offered different opportunities and challenges. The Life of Meresamun: A Temple Singer in Ancient Egypt, both the exhibit and the catalog, presents history through a sort of biography of an individual. The names of kings appear only as a background to the life of Meresamun, and we are invited instead to consider a woman in her professional capacity as a temple singer as well as in her roles as part of an elite household in Thebes, the religious capital of ancient Egypt. The context for her life comes from objects that define the life of women like Meresamun.

Unusual in this exhibit is the number of objects from our storerooms on display and the corresponding quantity of new photography prepared for the show. We are very pleased to recognize collaborations with Dr. Michael Vannier, Professor of Radiology at the University of Chicago Hospitals, as well as with professionals at Philips Healthcare. We were also fortunate to have the collegial assistance of graduate students in the Department of Near Eastern Languages and Civilizations at the University of Chicago.

It is a pleasure to join Gil Stein, Director of the Oriental Institute, in thanking the many people who have made this catalog and exhibit an extraordinary success.

Emily Teeter, exhibit curator and co-editor of the catalog, had the initial inspiration for the exhibit and has followed it through with creativity, energy, and intellectual curiosity.

Janet H. Johnson, co-editor of the catalog, provided the benefit of her extensive research on the social history of Late Period Egypt.

For financial support of the exhibit, we are all grateful to the extraordinary generosity of Rita and Kitty Picken.

Philips Healthcare, in particular Beverly Plost and Kimberly Miles, provided early access to their latest generation of CT scanners as well as significant financial support for the catalog. Their enthusiasm for the project made this a true collaboration, and generated interesting questions for us to address in the examination of radiological images.

We also acknowledge Exelon Corporation's extremely generous support of the Oriental Institute's Special Exhibit program.

The catalog editors join me in thanking:

Dianne Hanau-Strain, for her patience and her creative exhibit design.

Preparator Erik Lindahl and Assistant Preparator Brian Zimerle for their creative and helpful contributions.

Registrar Helen McDonald and especially Assistant Registrar Susan Allison for generating endless lists of objects and tracing their whereabouts as they passed through the various steps of conservation, photography, and installation.

Conservator Laura D'Alessandro and Assistant Conservator Alison Whyte, who were assigned the duties associated with this exhibit.

Especially warm thanks are extended to Photographer Anna Ressman, whose enthusiasm for each object was contagious and whose resulting images have greatly enhanced our image library. Thanks also to her assistants Kevin Bryce Lowry, Ian Randall, and Margaret Shortle. Other images of objects in the collection are the work of now-retired Oriental Institute photographer Jean Grant.

Museum Archivist John Larson was instrumental in searching out materials from our holdings, including the newly accessioned collection of photographs by the late Charles F. Nims.

Curatorial Assistant Tom James undertook a myriad of tasks for the project.

Museum intern Mary Cochran assisted with object and image research.

Sarah Sapperstein's deep familiarity with music was helpful in the finalization of that section of the catalog text.

Egyptology graduate students Jessica Henderson, Courtney Jacobson, Megaera Lorenz, and Elise MacArthur were a pleasure to work with, and we hope that their experience provided them with insights that might serve them in the future.

We also thank W. Raymond Johnson, Robert Ritner, and Hratch Papazian of the University of Chicago, Regina Schulz of the Walters Art Museum, and Terry Wilfong of the University of Michigan for their advice about specific objects or issues in the text.

The CT examination of the mummy could not have been done without the assistance of John Easton and expertise of Michael Vannier of the University of Chicago Hospitals.

Images in the catalog were provided with the assistance of Edward Bleiberg and Ruth Janson of the Brooklyn Museum; Mary Greuel and Jackie Maman of the Art Institute of Chicago; Chris Naunton of the Egypt Exploration Society, London; Deanna Cross of the Metropolitan Museum of Art; Christian Loeben and Christian Tepper of the Museum August Kestner in Hanover; Gabriele Pieke of the University of Bonn; and George B. Johnson. The photograph of Meresamun used on the front cover is the work of Dan Dry, commissioned by Suzanne Wilder of the University of Chicago Medical Center Communications Department.

Last, but so emphatically not least, our thanks are extended to the Oriental Institute's Publication Office. Tom Urban and Leslie Schramer were incredibly patient and supportive through a very tight deadline for preparation of the catalog. It is always a pleasure, and a valuable learning experience, to work with them.

CONTRIBUTORS

ABOUT THE CONTRIBUTORS:

JH   **Jessica Henderson** is a graduate student in the Department of Near Eastern Languages and Civilizations at the University of Chicago.

JHJ   **Janet H. Johnson** is the Morton D. Hull Distinguished Service Professor of Egyptology at the Oriental Institute and in the Department of Near Eastern Languages and Civilizations and in the Program on the Ancient Mediterranean World in the Department of Classics at the University of Chicago.

CDKJ   **Courtney DeNeice Kleinschmidt-Jacobson** is a graduate student in the Department of Near Eastern Languages and Civilizations at the University of Chicago.

ML   **Megaera Lorenz** is a graduate student in the Department of Near Eastern Languages and Civilizations at the University of Chicago.

EVM   **Elise V. MacArthur** is a graduate student in the Department of Near Eastern Languages and Civilizations at the University of Chicago.

HP   **Hratch Papazian** is a Lecturer in Egyptology in the Department of Near Eastern Languages and Civilizations at the University of Chicago.

ET   **Emily Teeter** is a Research Associate (Egyptology) and Coordinator of Special Exhibits at the Oriental Institute of the University of Chicago.

MV   **Michael Vannier** is a Professor of Radiology at the University of Chicago Hospitals and a pioneer in biomedical computer graphics. He serves as editor-in-chief of the *International Journal of Computer Aided Radiology and Surgery*.

IMAGE CREDITS:

Photography for Catalog Numbers 2, 10, 11, 12, 15, 56, 62, and back cover — Jean Grant; 63 — Tom van Eynde; front and inside covers — Dan Dry. All others by Anna Ressman.

Figures unless otherwise credited: 6, 15, 35, 38, 51 — Jean Grant; 23, 59 — Anna Ressman; 39 — Oriental Institute Archives; 41 — Oriental Institute Conservation Laboratory; 10–13, 60–77 — University of Chicago Medical Center; map by Leslie Schramer

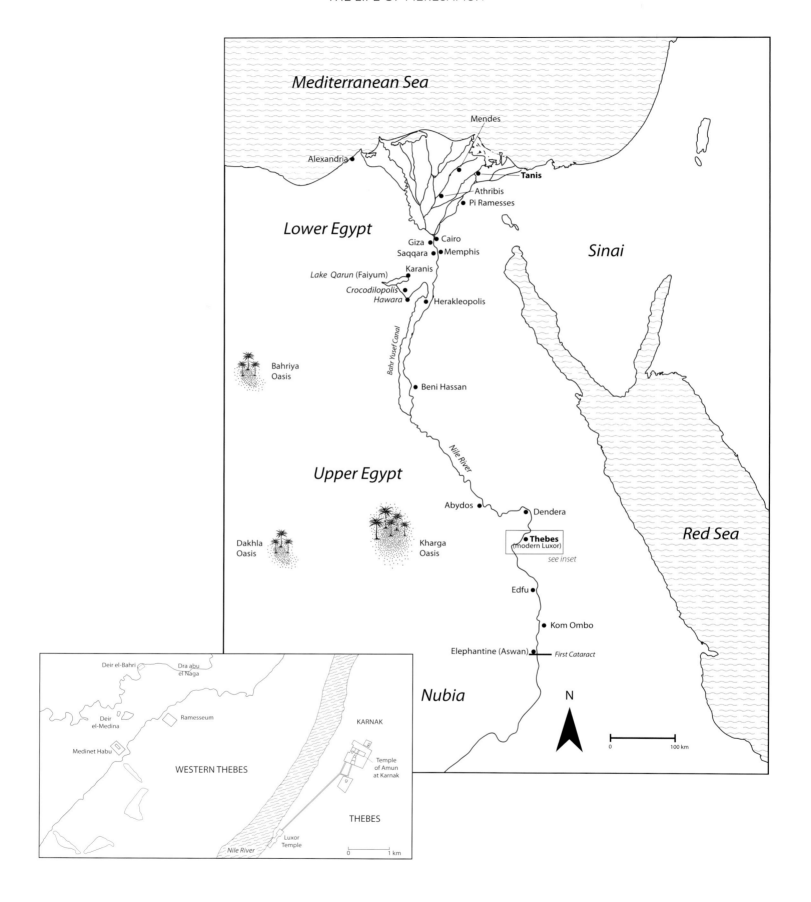

Map of Egypt

OUTLINE CHRONOLOGY

Dates are after *The Oxford History of Ancient Egypt*, edited by Ian Shaw (Oxford, 2000), and
The Third Intermediate Period in Egypt, by Kenneth A. Kitchen (Warminster, 1986).
Dates are B.C. unless otherwise indicated.

EARLY DYNASTIC PERIOD (DYNASTIES 1–2) 3000–2686

OLD KINGDOM (DYNASTIES 3–6) 2686–2181

FIRST INTERMEDIATE PERIOD (DYNASTIES 7–11) 2181–2055

MIDDLE KINGDOM (DYNASTIES 11–12) 2055–1773

SECOND INTERMEDIATE PERIOD (DYNASTIES 13–17) 1773–1550

NEW KINGDOM (DYNASTIES 18–20) 1550–1069

THIRD INTERMEDIATE PERIOD (DYNASTIES 21–24) 1069–715

    Dynasty 21 1069–945

    Dynasty 22 945–715

	Kings at Tanis		First Priests of Amun at Thebes
	Sheshonq I	945–924	Iuput (son of Sheshonq I)
	Osorkon I	924–889	Sheshonq (son of Osorkon I)
			Iuwelot (son of Osorkon I)
			Smendes (son of Osorkon I)
	Sheshonq II	ca. 890	Harsiese (son of Sheshonq II)
	Takelot I	889–874	
	Osorkon II	874–850	Nimlot (son of Osorkon II)
			Takelot (son of Nimlot)
	Takelot II	850–825	Prince Osorkon (son of Takelot II)
	Sheshonq III	825–773	Takelot (son of Nimlot?)
	Sheshonq V	767–730	Takelot (son of Osokon III of Dynasty 23)
	Osorkon IV	730–715	

    Dynasty 23 818–715

        Kings contemporary with late Dynasty 22, Dynasty 24, and early Dynasty 25

	Osorkon III	783–749	

    Dynasty 24 727–715

LATE PERIOD (DYNASTIES 25–31) 747–332

    Dynasty 25   Nubians rule Egypt, Assyrians sack Thebes at end of dynasty 747–656

    Dynasty 26   Kings ruling from Sais 664–525

    Dynasty 27   First Persian Period 525–359

    Dynasty 28   404–399

    Dynasty 29   399–380

    Dynasty 30   380–343

    Dynasty 31   Second Persian Period 343–332

PTOLEMAIC PERIOD   Conquest of Egypt by Alexander the Great in 332 332–30

ROMAN PERIOD . . . . 30 B.C.–A.D. 395

        (the Greco-Roman period comprises the Ptolemaic and Roman periods)

MERESAMUN'S EGYPT

EMILY TEETER

Meresamun was a woman who lived in ancient Egypt. We know Meresamun from her beautifully decorated coffin, which is now in the collection of the Oriental Institute (cat. no. 1). A single band of inscription running down the front of the coffin records her name and her job title: Singer in the Interior of the Temple of Amun, a type of elite musician-priestess. This position is associated with the Karnak temple in Thebes (modern Luxor), and so it is very probable that Meresamun lived in that city, which was the religious center of Egypt (see map, p. 12). This is disappointingly brief written documentation, but more evidence can be drawn from the coffin itself, for its style indicates that she lived about 800 B.C. With her name, her livelihood, and the time period in which she lived restored, we can use the rich corpus of contemporary texts and the archaeological record to create a biography of Meresamun.

HISTORICAL OUTLINE

By the reckoning of historians, Meresamun lived in the Twenty-second Dynasty during the Third Intermediate Period. During her life, Meresamun probably looked back in awe at the antiquity of her land. The pyramids were then nearly 2,000 years old, and pharaohs Thutmose III and Ramesses the Great were faintly remembered as being powerful rulers, their memory perpetuated by their architectural works and by their images on the walls of the temples.

Most of the Third Intermediate Period (Dynasties 21–24, about 1069–747 B.C.) was an era of political decentralization in the Nile Valley. The kings of the Twenty-first Dynasty (1069–945 B.C.) were Egyptianized military leaders of Libyan descent who ruled from the northern city of Tanis. The leaders in Thebes were army commanders who also held the title First Priest of Amun. The appointment of the First Priest was, in theory, the prerogative of the king in Tanis, although the Thebans were sometimes strong enough to appoint their own candidate. The ability of the Thebans to make their own determination of who would serve as First Priest served as a barometer of their independence.

For much of the Third Intermediate Period, the Nile Valley was ruled by several different contemporaneous dynasties (Dynasties 22–24) that were frequently at odds with each other. In the Twenty-second Dynasty, Thebes rose in revolt against the king in Tanis. The First Priest Nimlot was then the governor of southern Egypt. Upon the death of Nimlot, King Takelot II of Tanis (ruled 850–825 B.C.) exerted his control over the south by giving the post of Amun-Re in Thebes to his own son, Prince Osorkon. Osorkon, who held the titles general, army leader, and governor of southern Egypt, sailed south to Thebes to claim his office. He was initially greeted by the entire Theban priesthood, and he set about putting the temple and district administration in order. His actions included the execution of men who revolted against his authority. As recounted in the texts incised on the Bubastite Portal at the Karnak temple (fig. 1), each was "burned with fire in the place of [his] crime in Thebes." Afterward, Osorkon summoned the sons of the rebels and made each swear an oath of loyalty. That accomplished, he allowed each to assume the office of his dead father. Four years later, Thebes rebelled against Osorkon, a revolt that lasted a decade. Finally, Prince Osorkon made peace with the Thebans and traveled south to make offerings in the Amun temple at Karnak.

FIGURE 1. The Bubastite Portal at the Karnak temple. The gate was built by the rulers of Dynasty 22. The texts on the walls behind the pillars record the chronicles of Prince Osorkon in Thebes. Photo: Emily Teeter

Toward the end of the Twenty-second Dynasty, when Meresamun lived, the king at Tanis in the north was Sheshonq III, who reigned from 825 to 773 B.C. That the Thebans recognized Sheshonq as their king is shown by the fact that his name is surrounded by a cartouche (an indication of royalty) on statues and reliefs in Thebes. In an effort to maintain the peace, Sheshonq allowed Thebans to select their own First Priest of Amun. Within a few years, however, Sheshonq's power had eroded, for in texts that record the inundation level of the Nile he is referred to as co-ruler, having been forced to share his throne with his younger brother Pedubast. Meresamun could not have foreseen that the political situation would worsen after the time of her death, ultimately leading to such dramatic political fragmentation that, in about 747 B.C., the king of Nubia, Piye (formerly known as Piankhy), invaded Egypt. Piye and his successors created a vast kingdom that stretched from the Fifth Cataract of the Nile to the Mediterranean. The Nubian kings restored stability that in turn fostered a renaissance in building and the arts. But less than a century later they came into conflict with the Assyrians who, in 665 B.C., sacked Thebes and carried away the treasures of the city.

PRIESTS AND PRIESTESSES OF AMUN

The god Amun was the chief, but not the exclusive, god of the Thebans. His exalted status was indicated by his epithet "king of the gods." He was believed to reside in the temple of Amun at Karnak, as well as in Amun temples throughout the country. His temple at Karnak (fig. 2) was, and still is, one of the largest religious structures ever built, covering more than 100 hectares on the east bank of the Nile.

The god was all-powerful as the king himself, and in rare cases, the name "Amun" was enclosed in a cartouche as was customary for the living king. The god made known his will about administrative issues, such as appointments to government and temple offices, through oracles. But the god was also consulted on a wide variety of other matters such as the theft of property as well as small business matters (cat. nos. 15–16). These decisions were made when the god, in the form of a statue, left the temple in procession. Priests and members of the community presented yes/no questions to the statue of the god, which gave his judgments by movement or perhaps by sound (cat. no. 15).

FIGURE 3. The God's Wife of Amun, Shepenwepet, being crowned by the god Amun. From the chapel of Hekadjet at Karnak. Dynasty 23, ca. 783 B.C. Photo: Emily Teeter

FIGURE 2. View of the Bubastite Court of the Temple of Amun at Karnak, looking toward the earlier Second Pylon. The columns in the foreground are part of a kiosk built by the Nubian pharaoh Taharqa. Photo: Emily Teeter

Amun was served by an immense bureaucracy of priests and priestesses, administrators and clerks who managed the vast land holdings whose produce supported the temples of the god. Each day, hundreds of loaves of bread, jars of beer, baskets of fruit, incense, and lengths of cloth were laid upon gold and silver offering tables before the god. Offerings were left three times daily, and each involved a group of priests and their assistants, such as Meresamun, who officiated during the ritual.

Traditionally, the highest official of the Amun administration was the First Priest of Amun. By the time Meresamun began working in the temple, a princess who bore the title God's Wife [of Amun] or Adorer of the God had risen to power. About the time of Meresamun, the post was held by Shepenwepet (fig. 3), a daughter of King Osorkon III of the Twenty-third Dynasty. Shepenwepet and her successors were enormously influential and wealthy. In the period of Nubian domination (747–656 B.C.), they became the de facto rulers of the Theban area, governing on behalf of the pharaoh. Elite temple singers like Meresamun were shown in the presence of the God's Wife suggesting that they were close associates who assisted them with cult matters.

ARCHITECTURE, ART, AND LITERATURE IN THE TIME OF MERESAMUN

Traditionally, Egyptologists have not viewed the era in which Meresamun lived as a time of cultural achievement. Certainly the additions to the Karnak temple were modest and much of the renovation consisted of usurping the work of earlier rulers. The most ambitious project dates to the Twenty-second Dynasty, when Sheshonq I (ruled 945–924 B.C.) commissioned the huge Bubastite Court (80 x 100 meters) at Karnak, which enclosed earlier shrines. The gate in the southeast corner of the court was later embellished with texts and representations that record the struggles of Prince Osorkon with the Thebans. Later Nubian pharaohs built considerably more, especially Taharqa, who constructed an enormous kiosk in the Bubastite Court and an enigmatic Lake Edifice that served as a symbolic tomb of the sun. Beginning in the Twenty-third Dynasty, shortly after Meresamun's death, a series of small chapels to the god Osiris were built to the north of the Amun temple (figs. 4–5). These structures were dedicated by the king and the God's Wives to show the favor that the god showed to the rulers.

FIGURE 4A–B. The Chapel of Osiris-Onnophris in the Persea Tree at Karnak. The left side of the entry is carved with a scene of the God's Wife Amunirdis II embracing the god Amun, symbolizing their relationship. Dynasty 25, ca. 690 B.C. Photos: Emily Teeter

FIGURE 5A–B. The chapel of Osiris Hekadjet built by King Osorkon III. Among the reliefs are scenes of his daughter, the God's Wife of Amun Amunirdis, shaking ritual rattles (sistra). Dynasty 23, ca. 783 B.C. Photos: Emily Teeter

FIGURE 6. Block statue of Basa, a priest of Hathor, who is portrayed seated with his robe over his knees. His garment provides a surface for a long autobiographic inscription that recounts twenty-six generations of his family and records how priestly offices were handed down within generations of a single family. From Dendera. Dynasties 22–23, ca. 945–715 B.C. OIM 10729

It is in the smaller arts that the artists of the period excelled. "Block statues" that represent a man seated on the ground or on a small cushion, his cloak drawn over his knees (fig. 6), became one of the most popular forms of sculpture. The sides of the statue provided an ideal space for lengthy autobiographical inscriptions. Much of what is known about the period is recorded in these texts. There are very few block statues portraying women, and for unknown reasons, stone statues of any sort portraying females from this time are extremely rare.

Although most private tombs of the time of Meresamun are undecorated crypts that accommodated multiple burials, the contemporary coffins (fig. 7 and cat. no. 1) are among the most beautiful examples from any era. Typically, an inner coffin made of form-fitting cartonnage was enclosed in a series of two or three wood anthropoid coffins. Long papyri inscribed with texts from the Book of the Dead and with scenes of the deceased in the afterlife (fig. 8) were placed inside some of the coffins to serve as a sort of guidebook to the realm of the dead. Also typical of the period of Meresamun are painted wooden funerary stelae (cat. nos. 11, 62) that show the devotee offering to a deity, most often Re-Horakhty or Osiris. Women are frequently represented on these stelae, and they are a rich source for information on administrative titles and genealogical information, as well as clothing and hairstyles.

Another area of excellence was the field of bronze casting. Most statues in this material represent gods and goddesses (cat. no. 8), although several represent

God's Wives. Many of these served as offerings to gods (cat. nos. 19–20 and figs. 35–36), and some bear dedicatory inscriptions. The spectacular jewelry from the royal tombs at Tanis documents the apogee of metalworking incorporating elaborate stone and paste inlays. Many examples of fine faience, such as lotiform chalices, were also characteristic works of the time.

The Third Intermediate Period was also a period of literary achievement.[1] A wealth of autobiographical texts appear on block statues and stelae. One of the outstanding literary achievements of Egyptian literature, the Report of Wenamon, which relates the travels of an Egyptian trader to Lebanon, was composed during this time.

FIGURE 8. Section of the Book of the Dead for Tawy-henewt-Mut, Mistress of the House and Singer of the Temple of Amun-Re. She is shown adoring Osiris. Probably from Thebes. Dynasty 21, 1069–945 B.C. Art Institute of Chicago 1894.180. Photography copyright the Art Institute of Chicago

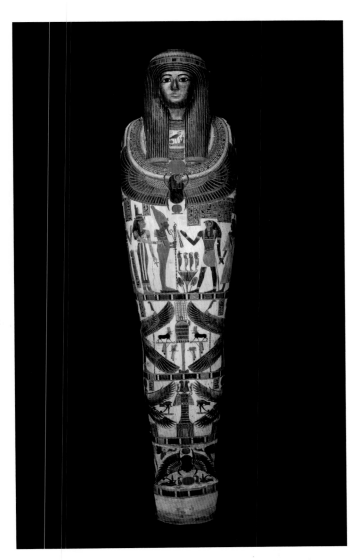

FIGURE 7. Cartonnage coffin of the Doorkeeper of the Temple of Amun, Paankhenamun. Probably from Thebes. Dynasty 22, ca. 945–715 B.C. Art Institute of Chicago 1910.238. Photography copyright the Art Institute of Chicago

Meresamun lived in a tumultuous but culturally rich time. Until recently, the unstable political situation led many scholars to discount the Third Intermediate Period as a time of decline and stagnation in comparison to the preceding New Kingdom with its famed kings and architectural achievements. Newer perspectives that look beyond monumental architecture to an appreciation of the small but elegant arts of metalworking, faience, and painting, however, reveal it as a time of innovation and excellence.

NOTE

[1] For a new compendium of texts from this era, see Ritner, *Libyan Anarchy*.

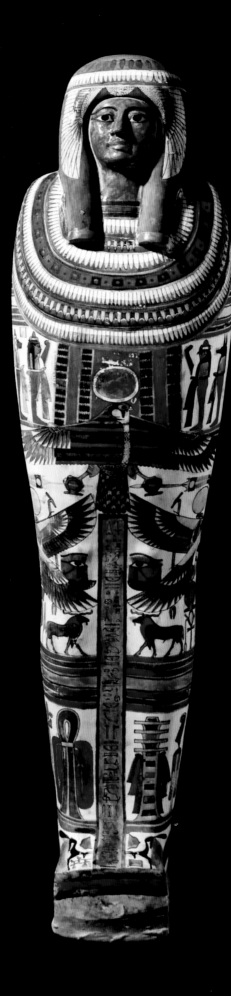

1. COFFIN AND MUMMY OF MERESAMUN

Cartonnage (fabric, glue, plaster), linen, pigment, human remains
Third Intermediate Period, Dynasty 22, ca. 945–715 B.C.
Purchased in Egypt, 1920
L: 160 cm
OIM 10797

Meresamun is known from her coffin and mummy. Her identity is established by the brief inscription on the coffin that states her name and gives her title: Singer in the Interior of the Temple of Amun. The coffin was purchased, and so nothing is known about her tomb, its location, or other funerary goods.

However, a great amount of general information can be gleaned from the coffin and mummy. The style of this coffin is characteristic of the Twenty-second Dynasty, establishing the era in which Meresamun lived. This type of coffin, which was expensive, indicates that she was from a wealthy family. It was only one element of a set that originally included one or two wood anthropoid coffins into which the inner coffin was nested (fig. 9). This privileged economic standing of Meresamun's family is echoed by her priestly title, Singer in the Interior of the Temple of Amun. Other women who held this title are known to have been the sisters or daughters of kings, governors, mayors, and high priests. Unfortunately, the name of her parents is not included in the brief inscription, making it impossible to reconstruct her genealogy.

FIGURE 9. This set of coffins belonged to Shepet-en-Khonsu, a Mistress of the House who lived in Thebes in Dynasty 22. Her cartonnage coffin (*right*) was nested inside a wood coffin, which in turn was enclosed in a larger outer coffin (*left*). Meresamun's set of coffins would have been similar. Oriental Institute excavations at the tomb of Kheruef, 1957–1958. Photo: Oriental Institute

Meresamun's title indicates that she lived and worked in Thebes, the main cult center of the god Amun, and that she worked in the temple of Amun at Karnak. Her personal name, Meresamun, which can be translated "Amun-Loves-Her," also suggests a Theban origin, because it symbolically placed her under the protection of the Theban deity.

The coffin is made of cartonnage composed of layers of fabric, thin plaster, and glue, much like papier-mâché. It was formed over a temporary inner core made of mud and straw. After the coffin shell was completed, the core was scraped out through an opening that runs from the head to the foot of the case. The wrapped mummy was then inserted into the case, the back seam was closed with lacing, and a separate footboard made of several pieces of wood was attached to the case. The entire coffin was covered with another layer of thin white plaster and then painted. The colored areas were painted with a final layer of protective varnish that has turned yellow with age. The coffin has never been opened.

The coffin portrays Meresamun wearing the vulture headdress that was worn by priestesses as well as by other women of high rank. A tiny vulture head is on her forehead and the bird's wings sweep down

1, detail of lower legs of the coffin, showing the Isis knot opposite the djed *pillar*

1, detail of head and chest of the coffin. The head of the vulture is barely visible in the half circle on her forehead

both sides of her face. Her chest is covered with a representation of floral collars. The Four Sons of Horus, the guardians of the organs that were removed in the process of mummification, are depicted below the collars. Each carries a strip of cloth, perhaps a reference to the mummification process, and a feather, the emblem of "truth" or justification in the afterlife. Below these gods is a large representation of the falcon god Re with the sun's disk on his head, clasping the šn hieroglyph (⌀ "eternity") in each talon. Re symbolizes the unending cycle of the rising and setting of the sun that was equated with eternal rebirth.

On either side of the central band on the leg area of the coffin are *wedjat* eyes, which symbolized health and regeneration. Behind the eyes are winged serpents with sun disks on their heads — symbols of protection. The serpent to the right hovers above the hieroglyphs for eternity, life, and dominion. Below the serpents are rams, which may be a pun on the word "soul" (the words "soul" and "ram" sounded the same in the ancient Egyptian language). Or the ram may represent the god Khnum, one of the primary creator gods, or Ba-neb-djed, who was associated with the soul of Osiris, one of the deities of the afterlife.

The large-scale hieroglyphs on the lower leg area are the *djed* pillar, which symbolized the backbone of the god Osiris, the main deity of the afterlife, and the *tiet*, so-called Isis knot, a symbol with broad meaning, associated generally with health and well-being. Two images of the jackal god Wepwawet, protector of the necropolis, decorate the upper surface of the feet. The footboard of the coffin is decorated with a gamboling calf, which, on other coffins, is identified as the god Apis.

The mummy within the coffin is of a woman about thirty years old.

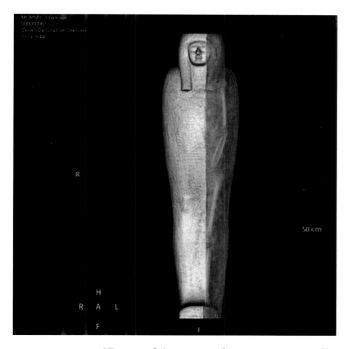

FIGURE 10. CT image of the mummy of Meresamun in its coffin

1, detail of the footboard of the coffin

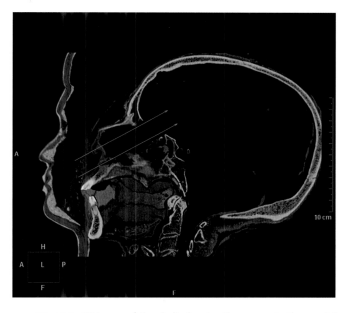

FIGURE 11. CT image of the skull, showing the access to the cranial cavity through the sinus (indicated by green lines) and the tentorium

THE MUMMIFICATION OF MERESAMUN

The mummy was prepared with the arms placed along the sides of the body, the hands over the pubis (fig. 10). The head is positioned slightly upward with the chin nearly touching the interior of the cartonnage case. The brain was removed through the ethmoid sinus. Unusual care was taken when the brain was removed, for the structure that separates the section of the brain (tentorium) was preserved (figs. 11, 76). No resin or other material was introduced into the cranium. The orbits are covered with eye-shaped pieces of dense material, probably stone or faience (fig. 12). The mouth was filled with a dense substance (fig. 13).

The embalmer's incision, as usual, is on the left side of the abdomen. It is covered with wadded linen. The abdomen has been packed with a granular material and with loose wads of linen. This linen packing was inserted far up in the chest cavity. A large mass of unidentified granular material is present at the throat (fig. 13).[1] In the 1991 CT

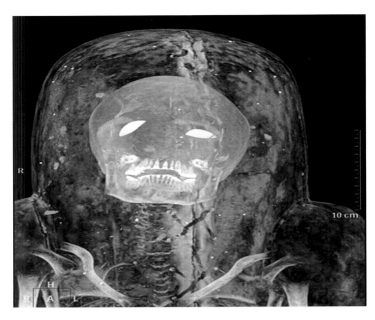

FIGURE 12. CT image of the head, with objects over the eyes

examination, this mass was tentatively identified as a goiter, but with the better resolution of the October 2008 examinations, it appears to be material introduced by the embalmers, probably under the skin.

A large quantity of linen was used for the preparation of the mummy (fig. 13). Wads of loosely gathered textile are bunched around the shoulders, between the legs and behind the shoulders. As is normal for Egyptian mummies, the limbs are wrapped separately and then wrapped to the body with multiple layers of linen. A material, perhaps resin, was applied to the wrappings before additional layers were added, leaving a dense layer between them.

Previous scans failed to detect any amulets or jewelry. In the most recent study, however, two small rectangular objects, perhaps faience amulets, were detected. One is on the breast and the other is near the small of the back. The latter appears to be outside the final layer of wrappings. The absence of beaded jewelry or other amulets on a mummy of this apparent quality is surprising.

There is ongoing scholarly debate whether women who held the title "Singer in the Interior of the Temple" were, on account of their temple duties, celibate. One specific goal of the most recent CT examination was to determine whether Meresamun had given birth through an examination of the pelvic symphysis. The evidence was inconclusive. See *Radiological Report on the Mummy of Meresamun*, below, pp. 110–17, for more about the CT scan of Meresamun.   ET

PUBLISHED

Teeter, *Ancient Egypt*, no. 38.

NOTE

[1] See similar treatment on the mummy of Nesperennub in Taylor, *Mummy: The Inside Story*, p. 23.

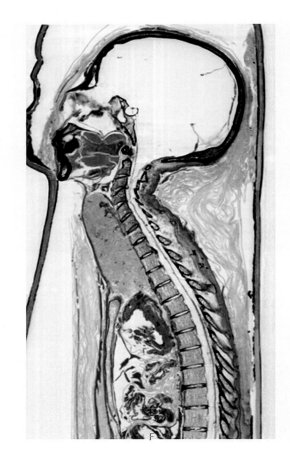

FIGURE 13. CT image of the head, neck, and spine of Meresamun, showing a mass of material at the throat and in the mouth, loosely wadded linen behind the head, and packing in the chest

INSIDE THE TEMPLE:
THE ROLE AND FUNCTION OF TEMPLE SINGERS

EMILY TEETER

See her, her hands shaking the sistra to bring pleasure to the god, her father Amun. How lovely she moves, her hair bound with ribbon, songstress with perfect features.... Pleasure there is in her lip's motions.... Her heart is all kindness, her words gentle to those upon earth. One lives just to hear her voice....[1]
— Description of Queen Nofertari as a temple singer in the Luxor temple

As a Singer in the Interior of the Temple of Amun, Meresamun belonged to a group of elite musician-priestesses who sang and made music for the god Amun. Music played an important role in Egyptian religion. The gods, who had many of the same characteristics as humans, were thought to be entertained by music. Moreover, music made by the ritual rattle (sistrum) and beaded necklace (menat) could calm the gods and make them more amenable to protecting and helping mankind. As related by a text from about 1325 B.C., the temple singer was one "who pacifies the god with a sweet voice...."[2] Singers in the time of Meresamun were an important part of the temple staff, as indicated by the large number of women who held musician-priestess titles.

Evidence for the temple singers is drawn mainly from paintings and reliefs in temples and tombs (fig. 14), and from genealogies that appear on coffins and stelae.

HISTORICAL DEVELOPMENT OF TEMPLE SINGERS

The earliest known evidence of temple singers is found on reliefs in tombs of the Old Kingdom (ca. 2500 B.C.). In that period, with few exceptions,[3] they bore the title *heset* (ḥst) "singer," and they were exclusively female. Many of the singers were part of an institution called the *khener* (ḥnr) (see cat. no. 10), a professional troupe of dancers and singers associated with the goddesses Bat, Hathor, Wepwawet, and Horus. By the middle of the Old Kingdom, the *khener* included men. In the late Middle Kingdom, a new class of singer-priestesses called *shemayet* (šmˁyt) appeared. The difference in their musical duties is unclear.

By the New Kingdom, great numbers of female singers who bore the title *heset* or *shemayet*, and even princesses and queens, are shown shaking sistra as temple musicians. In the early New Kingdom (Dynasty 18), the singers were drawn from the most elite families and many of them were married to priests, although husband and wife did not necessarily serve the same deity. During the Nineteenth and Twentieth Dynasties, the singers hailed from less elevated and more diverse backgrounds, judging by their husbands, who were scribes, laundrymen, and military men rather than priests.[4]

In the Third Intermediate Period when Meresamun lived, the women who bore the title Singer in the Interior of the Temple of Amun came from the highest strata of society. Several were princesses or the daughters of the mayor of Thebes.[5] Even the lowest levels of

FIGURE 14. A woman (*right*) sings to the sound of a flute, and two women (*left*) dance a "pantomime" during the celebration of the jubilee (Sed) festival of Amunhotep III. Relief in the tomb of Kheruef (Theban Tomb 192). New Kingdom, Dynasty 18, reign of Amunhotep III, ca. 1352 B.C. Photo: C. F. Nims

singers, the simple *shemayet* from elite families, were so numerous that it seems that most households had members who were singers. The tradition of temple musicians continued into the Ptolemaic and Roman periods, although the particular title held by Meresamun seems to have fallen out of use in about 650 B.C. In the New Kingdom and later, the gods most commonly served by the priestesses were Amun, Montu, Isis, Mut, and Osiris.

FIGURE 15. Fragment from the tomb of the Singer in the Interior of the Temple of Amun, Diesehebsed (*left*). She is shown with the God's Wife Amunirdis II. Dynasty 25, ca. 670 B.C. From Medinet Habu. OIM 14681

ORGANIZATION AND PAYMENT OF TEMPLE SINGERS

We do not know how many singers served in an individual temple, much less in the enormous temple of Amun at Karnak where Meresamun probably worked. Lists of titles indicate that there were several types of temple singers. In the time of Meresamun, the most common titles for temple singers were various grades of *shemayet*. Other titles include *heset* "singer" and various types of sistrum players (*shmyt, sššyt,* and *ihywt*). It is not known how the sistrum players' duties were differentiated from the singers who appear with sistra. Another title, *shespet dekhen* (*sspt dhn*), was the designation for a musician choir, usually male, who kept the beat and who is seen mainly in festival scenes outside the temple and in scenes from tombs.

Meresamun and her musician colleagues were organized into ranks. Like other categories of priests,

the singers were organized into four groups termed *sȝ*, known by the Greek name phyles, that served one month out of four. After serving for the requisite month of thirty days, Meresamun would not have returned to temple duty until next rotation of duty ninety days later. The phyles were supervised by an Overseer of the Phyles (*ḥry sȝ*).

Each rank of singers had its own overseer. The *shemayet*-singers were overseen by the Great Singer (*šm'yt wrt*) or by the Overseer of the Singers (*ḥry šm'yt*), while the Singers in the Interior of the Temple of Amun, like Meresamun, were overseen by the Great Singer in the Interior of the Temple of Amun (*wrt ḥry n ḥnw n Imn*).[5] The ultimate supervisor of singers would have been either the Divine Adoratress of Amun (also called the God's Wife) (figs. 15–16)[7] or the First Priest of Amun of Karnak, who were the two most influential officials in Thebes and who bore the responsibility of managing the vast wealth of Amun.

The Restoration Stela of Tutankhamun (ca. 1334 B.C.), although from an era earlier than Meresamun, indicates that singers and dancers assigned to the renovated temples were paid from the palace account. Although we have no direct evidence, it seems very likely that the singers, like the priests for whom we have better documentation, received a portion of the offerings laid before the god. To give an idea of the amount of food that circulated through the temple, one set of the many offering tables of King Ramesses III at the

FIGURE 16. The God's Wife of Amun Shepenwepet II offering wine jars to Osiris. Behind her, in much smaller scale, is the Singer in the Interior of the Temple of Amun, Diesehebsed. The singers were under the supervision of the God's Wives. Chapel of Osiris-Onnophris in the Persea Tree at Karnak, Dynasty 25, ca. 747–716 B.C. Photo: Emily Teeter

Karnak temple received twenty sacks of grain offerings daily (equivalent to 1,500 liters), the annual total being enough to support 110 families.[8] This was supplemented by vast amounts of fruits, vegetables, meat, and fowl (see cat. no. 14).

We have scant information about what the temple singers did when not working in the temple. Some were women of considerable authority. Herere, a singer with the supervisory title Great One of the *khener* and Singer of Amun-Re, wrote sharply to a troop commander ordering him to supply rations for workmen in Thebes, warning him: "Don't let [a certain official] ... complain to me again. Have them prepared [for] people...." Hennuttawy, another singer of Amun, wrote a letter indicating that, at the request of the necropolis scribe, she had intervened in the grain deliveries to the temple: "I went myself and caused the grain to be received while I was there."[9]

TRAINING OF TEMPLE SINGERS

Very little is known about the training of temple musicians. However, it is very likely that girls learned the job from their mothers, for often several generations of women in a single family held the same title. For example, fourteen women of the family of Tjaynefer at Thebes (ca. 1200 B.C.) bore the title *shemayet* "singer" and there are several mother-daughter pairs who bore the prestigious title Singer in the Interior of the Temple of Amun.[10] The mummy of a little girl who held the title Singer of Amun indicates that one could perform in temples as a youth.[11] During the time of Meresamun it

was exceedingly common for sons to inherit the priestly office of their father, and it seems quite likely that the singer-priestesses followed the same pattern.

One hint about the appointment of singers, although from five hundred years before Meresamun, appears on the Restoration Stela of Tutankhamun. The text mentions that singers who had worked in the palace were appointed to the renovated temples.[12]

Meresamun would have started at the lower rank of Singer, advancing to Singer in the Temple, and finally to the rank that allowed her access into the more sacred areas near the statue of the deity. The position of temple singer was so prestigious that women with the title tended to use it in preference to other titles that they held.

DUTIES AND RESPONSIBILITIES OF TEMPLE SINGERS

Meresamun and her colleagues served as a divine choir that accompanied the First Priest as he performed his rituals. The main rite performed inside the temple of Amun (as well as in temples dedicated to other deities) was an elaborate offering ceremony that maintained the god who, in the form of a precious statue, dwelled in the temple's sanctuary. Three times a day, a priest, accompanied by singers and other attendants, would ceremonially open the doors of the sanctuary, purify the divine statue, offer it food and beverages, and adorn it with clothing, jewelry, and perfumes. Heaps of food were laid before the statue to nourish the deity.

Singer-priestesses also entertained when the resident god left the temple to visit other temples and to

FIGURE 17. Queen Iset(?), holding sistra (*left*), leads a procession of Singers of Amun with their sistra and menats during the festival of Opet in Thebes. Dynasty 20, ca. 1184–1153 B.C. From Karnak. Epigraphic Survey, *Reliefs and Inscriptions at Karnak*, vol. 2, pl. 88

give oracles (see cat. nos. 15–16). Scenes of musician-priestesses officiating outside the temple document these activities. In the annual Opet Festival, during which Amun traveled from the Karnak temple to the Luxor temple, the procession was greeted by the queen who shook two sistra. Behind her was a group of seven women, labeled "Singers of Amun," who hold menats and shake sistra before the boat that carried the god (fig. 17). As the boat carrying the god returned to Karnak, temple singers with sistra and menats performed near a man with a large double-ended drum slung around his neck and a group of Libyans with clap sticks (fig. 18, and see cat. no. 3). In another scene from the festival, three temple musicians "of the *khener* of the temple," with their sistra and menats, performed in conjunction with a larger group composed of a harpist, three men who clap their hands to keep the beat, male dancers, and a group of acrobatic female dancers who do back flips and throw their hair over their faces (fig. 19).

Musicians were also present during the Sed Festival that commemorated the thirtieth anniversary of the king's accession. One sequence of the festival involved the raising of a large *djed* pillar that symbolized the resurrection of Osiris and rejuvenation of the king. As shown in the tomb of Kheruef at Thebes (ca. 1350 B.C.), princesses holding a naos sistrum and a menat sing or chant, "To your spirit, the sistrum to your beautiful face, the menat necklaces and sistra as you arise O august *djed* pillar..." (fig. 20). In another sequence, a pair of women labeled "Singer" play a frame drum. They are followed by three pairs of women who clap out the rhythm for four dancers. This tradition persisted well into the time of Meresamun, for Singers of the Temple of Amun and sistrum players (*iḥywt*) are shown performing at the Sed Festival of Osorkon II.[13]

Women holding or shaking sistra are also seen in tomb scenes. In the Old Kingdom, before the appearance of the title *shemayet*, the female and male singers shown in tombs bear the title Singer (*ḥst* or *ḥsi*). They are often shown in groups that include dancers

FIGURE 18. Musicians at the Opet Festival. The troupe is led by three men with lutes, a group of Libyans with clap sticks, men who clap to the beat, and a man with a large drum. From the Luxor temple, Dynasty 18, ca. 1330 B.C. Epigraphic Survey, *Festival Procession of Opet*, pl. 91

FIGURE 19. A harpist plays, musicians from the *khener* shake sistra, and men clap the rhythm as acrobatic dancers perform during the Opet Festival in Thebes. From the Chapelle Rouge of Hatshepsut, Dynasty 18, ca. 1460 B.C. Photo: Oriental Institute

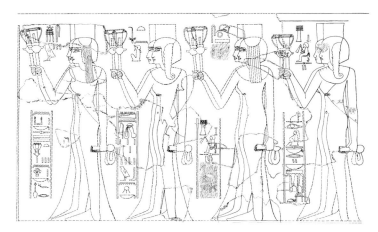

FIGURE 20. Princesses with their sistra and menats at the Sed Festival. From the tomb of Kheruef (Theban Tomb 192). Dynasty 18, reign of Amunhotep III, ca. 1352 B.C. Epigraphic Survey, *Tomb of Kheruef*, pl. 57

of the *khener* (cat. no. 10). By the Middle Kingdom, groups of dancers and singers are smaller in number and consist mainly of women. A scene in the tomb of Amenemhet (Dynasty 11) depicting a woman playing a sistrum for the tomb owner is captioned "I offer to you (the deceased) the menat, the looped sistrum, the naos sistrum belonging to Amun, to the Ennead and to Hathor in all her names, that they may grant you a fair and long-lasting life," indicting that the musician's actions ensured an eternal life after death.

By the New Kingdom, when gods are shown in private tombs, the wife of the tomb owner is often shown standing behind her husband (fig. 21). As he raises his hands in adoration of the god, she shakes a sistrum and holds her other hand in a salute of honor. Here, the sistrum is the archetypal symbol of how a woman approached the deity and placated him or her with music.

Very rarely, temple singers are shown singing and shaking sistra outside a temple or festival setting. In a scene in his tomb, Rekhmire, the mayor of Thebes, returns from a meeting with the king. He was greeted by eleven daughters or granddaughters, each of whom is identified as a Singer of Amun.[14] Six of them actively shake sistra, while five hold a sistrum in a passive pose. Seven of them also hold menats or drape them over their arms.

Women who held titles indicating their association with ritual music are very common throughout the dynastic period, attesting to the important role that music played in all manifestations of religion. The daily offering service that cared for the gods and goddesses of Egypt, the myriad public festivals and processions, as well as mortuary ceremonies all incorporated ritual musicians.

NOTES

[1] Foster, *Echoes of Egyptian Voices*, pp. 61–62.

[2] Teeter, "Female Musicians," p. 86, n. 93.

[3] For a single attestation of a *shemayet* in the Old Kingdom, see Onstine, *Role of the Chantress*, p. 65.

[4] Ibid., p. 36.

[5] Meresamunet, daughter of Osorkon, Sheamamunimes, mother of Meresamunet and daughter of the Chief of the Meswesh Takelot (II) (both in Ritner, "Oblique Reference," pp. 352–53); Nester, daughter of King Amunrud (Hölscher, *Excavation*, vol. 5, p. 32); Diesehebsed, sister of the mayor of Thebes Montuemhat; Diesehebsed; daughter of the mayor of Thebes (Teeter, "Diesehebsed," p. 196).

[6] Naguib, *Le clergé féminine*, p. 224.

[7] For the singers being subordinate to the Divine Adoratress, see the Tomb Robbery papyrus, where four *shemayet* are "of the estate of the Divine Adoratress" (*n pr n dwȝ ntr*). Onstine, *Role of the Chantress*, p. 21.

[8] Haring, *Households*, 1997, p. 92.

[9] Wente, *Letters*, 1990, pp. 200–01, 174.

[10] Teeter, "Female Musicians," p. 86, n. 93.

[11] Onstine, *Role of the Chantress*, p. 9, no. 144.

[12] Murnane, *Texts from the Amarna Period*, p. 214.

[13] Naville, *Festival Hall*, pls. 5, 14, 25.

[14] Davies, *Tomb of Rekh-Mi-Rē*, pls. 70, 71.

FIGURE 21. Nakhtamun and his wife Kemena approach Hathor in the form of a cow emerging from the western hills of Thebes. Nakhtamun raises his hands in adoration as Kemena shakes her sistrum. From the tomb of Nakhtamun (Theban Tomb 341). New Kingdom, Dynasty 20, ca. 1250 B.C. Photo: C. F. Nims

RITUAL MUSIC

Emily Teeter

Meresamun and her colleagues were part of a group of musician-priestesses who performed during religious rituals and festivals. Music in ancient Egypt played an important role in religious practice because it was thought to please and soothe the gods and to dispel evil. The instruments most closely associated with music played in temples are the sistrum and the menat.

A sistrum is a rattle that was played primarily by queens, princesses, and priestesses in the course of offering rituals and sacred processions. The goddess Hathor, who was known as the Mistress of Music, was so strongly associated with the sistrum that her face decorated the handle of most examples. The sistrum is also connected to the worship of Hathor through a ritual called "plucking papyrus for Hathor" (fig. 22 and cat. no. 51), apparently because the sound of the sistrum was equated with the rustling sound that papyrus made in the marsh. This equation was further stressed by a pun, for both "sistrum" and "plucking" were *sesheshet* (*sššt*) in the ancient Egyptian language, and both words were onomatopoetic.

The act of shaking a sistrum was also thought to protect the goddess and her subjects. This protection is made clear by scenes at the temple of Hathor at Dendera that are captioned: "I have taken the *sesheshet* sistrum, I

grasp the sistrum and drive away the one who is hostile to the Mistress of Heaven" (Hathor) and "I dispel what is evil by means of the sistrum in my hand."[1]

Sistra are known from the Old Kingdom and they continue to be an important part of temple equipment into the Roman period. They are shown in religious scenes well into the Christian period, and a form of sistrum is still used in the liturgy of the Coptic (Egyptian) church. The English word "sistrum" is derived from the Greek *seiein* "to shake."

There are two forms of sistra. The looped, or arched, sistrum is characterized by the curved band of metal that supports the three or four crossbars that are fitted with metal tangs or disks. A face of Hathor appears at the upper part of the handle below the arch (cat. no. 4). This style of sistrum, known as the *sekhem* or *ib*, is usually made of bronze.

The other form of rattle, called the naos (shine-shaped) sistrum, or *sesheshet* (fig. 23), appeared in the Old Kingdom and continued to be used into the Roman era. On this type, the face of

FIGURE 22. Votive bed decorated with a scene of the ritual of plucking papyrus for Hathor. A musician playing a lute is seated in a boat. A woman (*left*) punts the boat through the marsh while another in the bow (*right*) plucks papyrus. The sound of the rustling papyrus was equated with the sound of a sistrum. The imagery of the naked women, a musician, and figures of Bes that flank the composition all refer to Hathor. Drawing of Cairo JdE 59845 by Angela Altenhofen

FIGURE 23. Faience naos-type sistrum. Late Period, Dynasty 26, reign of Amasis, 570–526 B.C. OIM 10718

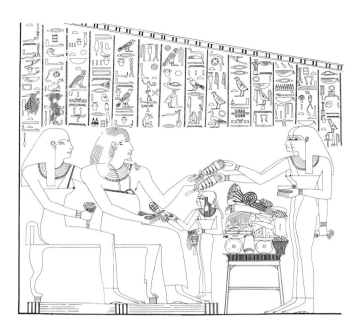

FIGURE 24. The protective qualities of ritual musical instruments is illustrated by scenes such as this where sistra are presented to the deceased. From the tomb of Rekhmire (Theban Tomb 100), Dynasty 18, ca. 1427 B.C. After Davies, *Tomb of Rekh-Mi-Rē'*, pl. 63

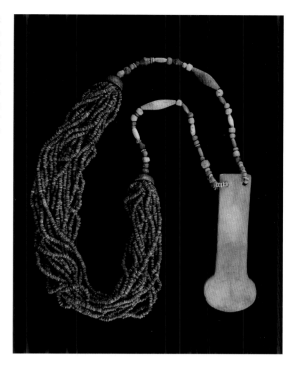

FIGURE 25. Menat necklace of faience. Provenance unknown. Late Period, 6th–3rd century B.C. BoSL 1634. Photo courtesy of the Ägyptisches Museum der Universität Bonn

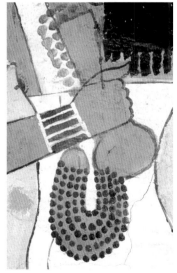

FIGURE 26. The Mistress of the House and Singer of Amun, Mery, her menat gathered in her hand (*detail*). In her other hand she holds her sistrum by the loop. Tomb of Sennefer (Theban Tomb 96), Dynasty 18, ca. 1400 B.C. Photo: C. F. Nims

Hathor is surmounted by a representation of a doorway of a naos. The transverse bars that support the jingles cross the doorway. Most naos sistra are made of faience.

There does not seem to be a functional or symbolic difference between the two types of rattles. Often musicians have a looped sistrum in one hand and a naos-type in the other (see cat. no. 2). In temple reliefs, musicians may be shown holding one style of sistrum in some scenes and the other style in other reliefs, with no clear reason for the choice.

Sistra are also shown in funerary scenes, where they are associated with granting the deceased a happy afterlife (fig. 24). A scene in the tomb of Amenemhet where sistra and menat are offered to the deceased is captioned: "I offer to you (the deceased) the menat, the looped sistrum, the naos sistrum belonging to Amun, to the Ennead and to Hathor in all her names, that they may grant you a fair and long-lasting life."

The menat was a multi-strand beaded necklace attached to a metal, stone, or faience counterpoise (figs. 25–26). The menat necklace was carried by the counterpoise, gathered in the hand, held in one hand with a sistrum, draped over the elbow, over the shoulder, or worn as a conventional necklace. When shaken, it made a swishing sound that, like the sistrum, may have been associated with the sound of papyrus in the marsh. The menat is almost entirely associated with females,[2] although for unknown reasons it is the characteristic necklace of the god Khonsu.

When musicians moved outside the temple proper, as was the case during festivals, a wider range of instruments is shown, including round or rectangular frame drums, harps (cat. no. 9), lutes, and a large double-ended drum. The frame drum and the harp were played by both men and women. Lutes, lyres, oboes, and flutes seen in banqueting scenes were not used in temple ritual until the Greco-Roman period.

The apparent absence of any form of musical notation makes it impossible to reconstruct the tones or rhythms of Egyptian music.[3] As a result, our knowledge is based upon representations of musicians in temples and tombs and the musical instruments themselves. It has been suggested that the form of singing accompanied by the sistrum and menat (which have virtually no range of tone) was chanting rather than lyric song.[4] However, several scenes of women bearing the title Singer or Singer of Amun include what seem to be lyrics. These can be very brief stanzas such as "To your *ka*, the sistrum to your beautiful face, the menat necklaces and *sekhem* sistra as you arise O august *djed* pillar...." But much longer sets of lyrics are recorded for some of the great festivals at Thebes. The lyrics sung by the priestesses and priests during the annual Opet Festival, when Amun left the Karnak temple to visit the Luxor temple, are recorded on the walls of the latter temple. This song was accompanied by sistrum and menat:

> O Amun-Re, Lord of the Thrones of the Two Lands, may you live forever! A drinking place is hewn out, the sky is folded back to the south, [a drinking place] is hewn out, the sky is folded back to the north, that the sailor of [King] Horemheb, beloved of Amun-Re-Kamutef, praised of the gods may drink!

> Hail Amun-Re, the primeval one of the two lands, foremost one of Karnak, in your glorious appearance amidst your [river] fleet, in your beautiful festival of Opet, may you be pleased with it. A drinking place is built for the party which is in the (best) ship of ships(?). The paths of the Akeru [east–west horizons] are bound up for you; a great Inundation is raised up. May you pacify the Two Ladies, O lord of the red [and] white crown, Horus strong of arm, while the god is conveyed with her, the good one of the god, (and) after Hathor has done the most wonderful of things for Horemheb, beloved of Amun, praised one of the gods.[5]

The song performed during the annual Festival of the Valley, in which Amun left his temple and traveled through the necropoleis, contains the following lyrics:

> O Amun, the heaven is uplifted for you; the ground is trodden for you. Ptah with his two hands makes a chapel as a resting place for your heart....

> How great is Amun, the beloved god! He rises in Karnak, his city, the Lord of Life.... The beautiful face of Amun, the beloved power, at whom the gods love to look, as the mighty one who came forth from the horizon! The whole entire land of Amun's domain is in festival. It is happy for Amun-Re, it is he whom mankind loves."[6]

The Sed Festival that commemorated the thirtieth anniversary of the king's rule was celebrated with the following song in honor of Hathor, who played a prominent role in the festivities:

> Come! Make jubilation for The Gold [Hathor] and good pleasure for the Lady of the Two Lands that she may cause Neb-Maat-Re,[7] given life, to be enduring!

> Come! Arise! Come that I may make for you jubilation at twilight and music in the evening. O Hathor! You are exalted in the hair of Re, in the hair of Re, for to you has been given the sky, the deep night and the stars. Great is her majesty when she is happy.[8]

Even in the absence of the melodies, the richness of the imagery of the lyrics of temple music indicates that ritual music was a joyous adoration of the god.

NOTES

[1] Blackman, "Position of Women," pp. 158–59.

[2] Examples of kings with sistra include Ramesses II at Karnak (Helck, *Ritualszenen*, pl. 42) and Ptolemy III at Karnak (Clère, *Porte d'Évergète*, pl. 25).

[3] See van Lieven, "Musical Notation," pp. 497–510, for the Roman-period Papyrus Carlsberg 589, with what may be a form of musical notation.

[4] Hickman, *Métier*, pp. 278–79; Teeter, "Female Musicians," p. 86, since reconsidered.

[5] Epigraphic Survey, *Festival Procession of Opet*, p. 12.

[6] Shorter, "Tomb of Aaḥmose," p. 57.

[7] The coronation name of Amunhotep III.

[8] Epigraphic Survey, *Tomb of Kheruef*, p. 47.

2. FAMILY OF TEMPLE MUSICIANS

Basalt
Early Ptolemaic period (Macedonian Dynasty),
reign of Philip Arrhidaeus, 323–317 B.C.
Purchased in Egypt, 1919
H: 32.0; L: 56.2; W: 33.5 cm
OIM 10589

Serving as a musician in a temple was a common
occupation for elite women, and often several
generations of women in a single family held that
position. One side of this statue base shows six
women of the family of a man named Djedhor. All
of them hold sistra, the primary instrument of a
temple musician. No specific titles are given for the
women, so we cannot tell what category of musician-
priestess they were, whether plain singers (šmʿyt) or
perhaps sistrum players (iḥywt) in the temple of the
falcon that Djedhor oversaw. Each woman carries two
different styles of sistra. The one in their left hand is
topped with a shrine-shaped structure (fig. 23), while
the one in their right hand is a looped sistrum with a
Hathor head (see cat. no. 4).

The image of the women and the accompanying
text reflect the high status of women in Egypt. Rather
than being marginal members of society, they are
prominently shown and depicted the same size as
their father and brothers, who are shown on the
opposite side of the statue base. The genealogical
information also stresses women's prominent role in
the culture. In the text near the figures, Djedhor's
own genealogy is given simply as "born of Ta-sherit
-(en)-taihet," without a reference to the name of his
father. It is only in the horizontal text that encircles
the top of the statue base that the name of his father,
Djedhor (Sr.), is given.

The first three women behind Djedhor are his
three daughters — Ta-sherit-(en)-taihet (Jr.), Khut,
and Ta-sherit-en-tayisw — by his wife Tayhesi, who
is shown immediately after her daughters. She bore
him the three girls as well as seven sons shown on
the opposite side of the statue base. The next figure
is a daughter named Bastet-iyw, born by another wife,
Tayhor, who is shown last. Non-royal Egyptians were
monogamous, so the procession shows two sequential
rather than concurrent wives. The position of Tayhesi
and her three daughters closer to Djedhor suggests
that she was the wife at the time the monument was

commissioned. Hence it seems likely that Tayhor was Djedhor's first wife who died or was divorced. If so, it is notable that her daughter Bastet-iyw is shown alongside her step-sisters, suggesting that Djedhor venerated all his children equally.

As is typical in Egyptian art, there was no attempt to differentiate stylistically the women from their daughters or to indicate the relative ages of the girls, although they may be presented in order of their birth. The musician-priestesses of Djedhor's family wear the same hairstyle and dress as that worn by any elite woman, whether priestess or not, indicating that priestesses were not visibly differentiated from other women.

The extensive text on the statue base relates the professional accomplishments of Djedhor in the sacred falcon yards in Athribis. The base once supported a statue of Djedhor, which, like another statue of him in Cairo, was covered with magical healing texts that protected against "the poison of every male and female viper and all snakes." Water would have been poured over the statue, magically absorbing the protective power of the spells. The liquid was then drunk as a cure for afflictions.   ET

PUBLISHED

Sherman, "Djedhor the Saviour Statue Base"; Teeter, *Ancient Egypt*, no. 52; Vernus, *Athribis*, p. 196, doc. 162; Young, "Consanguineous Marriage."

2, view of side

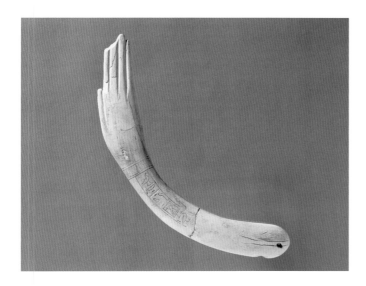

Most clap sticks have a hole bored through them that allowed a pair to be connected with a piece of fiber material. The string was placed around the wrist of the musician who struck the sticks together like castanets. An illustration of this can be seen in the tomb of Antefoqer and his wife Senet (fig. 27). Other pairs that were held separately in each hand are also depicted (fig. 28).

Clap sticks were used in a variety of settings, in temples to worship the gods as well as in festivals enacted outside the temple for the revivification of the king and in rituals in connection with the funerary meal of the deceased. They were used by both female and male musicians. There is also evidence that they were used by female members of the royal family. Two examples were found in the tomb of Tutankhamun (Dynasty 18) inscribed with the cartouches of Queen Tiy and Princess Meritaten.

This example was recovered from a private tomb. Where it was used, whether in funerary or temple rituals, is unknown. It has a bracelet design carved into the wrist as well as an inscription down the forearm which reads "female servant of the Princess Sit-Hathor," probably a princess of the Twelfth Dynasty. The mate to this clap stick is in the collection of the British Museum, London.

Despite the uncertainty about the function of this specific piece, clap sticks were an important aspect of music worship in temples and if Meresamun did not use one herself, it is very likely that she would have known and worked with people who did.   JH

3. CLAP STICK

Ivory
Middle Kingdom, Dynasty 12, ca. 1880 B.C.
Hu, grave Y 196
Gift of the Egypt Exploration Fund, 1899
OIM 5518

Clap sticks of this type were used in musical performances or rituals from the time of the early Old Kingdom. They were generally made of bone, ivory, or wood, and they are found in a variety of shapes. The most common, however, is in the general form of a human arm and hand. Many examples are also decorated with the head of Hathor, because she was regarded as the Mistress of Dance and the Mistress of Music. Although clappers were often used in rituals connected to Hathor, they are not specific to that goddess.

PUBLISHED

Petrie and Mace, *Diospolis Parva*, pl. 27, p. 53.

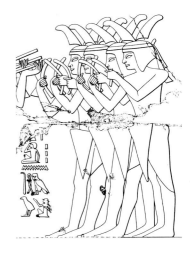

FIGURE 28. Libyans with clap sticks in the procession of the Opet Festival, when Amun of Karnak visited the Luxor temple. From the Colonnade Hall at Luxor. Dynasty 18, ca. 1330 B.C. Epigraphic Survey, *Festival Procession of Opet*, pls. 91, 99

FIGURE 27. Pairs of clappers looped around the hands of musicians. From the tomb of Antefoqer (Theban Tomb 60), Dynasty 12, reign of Senwosret I, ca. 1956–1911 B.C. From Davies, *Tomb of Antefoker*, pl. 23B. Courtesy of The Egypt Exploration Society, London

4, front

4, detail of back

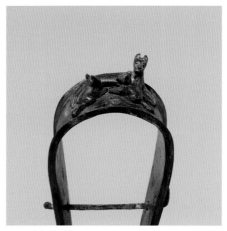

4, detail of top

4. SISTRUM

Bronze
Late Ptolemaic to Roman period, 3rd–1st century B.C.
Purchased in Berlin, 1933
H: 37.5; W: 8; Th: 5 cm
OIM 14058

A sistrum is a rattle that was played in religious processions and ceremonies. This example features a head of Hathor. Above the goddess is a tiny temple portal whose architraves are ornamented with recumbent lions. Crowned cobras rear up behind the lions. A standing figure of the potentially fierce feline, Bastet (see cat. no. 8), her head topped with a solar disk, stands in the doorway of the temple holding her sistrum. The three sides of the temple are detailed with double doors. A seated cat appears in front of the door on the left side of the little shrine, a crowned duck, the emblem of the god

Amun who is known as King of the Gods, on the right. The most benign form of feline — a cat nursing two kittens — appears on top of the sistrum.

The complex iconography on this sistrum alludes to one cycle of the Myth of the Eye of the Sun, in which Hathor, the daughter of Re, assumed the form of an angry lioness (or Nubian cat) who threatened to kill mankind because they rebelled against Re. Her anger was appeased by music.

The handle is in the form of the god Bes crowned with his feathered headdress. He stands on an open lily bloom flanked by two sphinxes. Bes and the lily are allusions to rebirth; Bes was the god who guarded women and children (see cat. nos. 51, 58), and the open lily symbolizes rebirth because the flower opens anew in the warm rays of the morning sun. The Greco-Roman form of the sphinxes, especially their recurved wings and their "melon" hairstyle, suggest the date for this object.   ET

5. RELIEF OF SISTRUM PLAYER

Sandstone, pigment
Dynasty 18, reigns of Amunhotep III–Horemheb,
ca. 1390–1295 B.C.
Luxor, Medinet Habu, temple of Aye and Horemheb
H: 23.6; W: 11.5; Th: 5 cm
OIM 14767

Walls of ancient Egyptian temples were usually
decorated with scenes of the activities that were
enacted in that space. This fragment shows a woman
shaking a sistrum with her right hand as she lifts her
left hand in an attitude of praise. The sistrum is the
loop type (cat. no. 4) with a handle topped by the
head of Hathor. The three crossbars that supported
the disks or tangs that made the percussive sound are
in the form of rearing serpents. Traces of distinctive
ribbons on the front of the sistrum player's gown
suggest that she is the queen, standing behind the
larger figure of the king. Other such scenes show
that they would have been standing before a god
(fig. 21). In such scenes the king normally approaches
the deity with offerings while the queen shakes a
sistrum.   ET

PUBLISHED

Hölscher, *Excavation of Medinet Habu*, vol. 2, pl. 43.i.

6. AEGIS

Bronze, pigment
Third Intermediate–Late Period, Dynasties 22–26,
ca. 945–525 B.C.
Purchased in Egypt, 1920
H: 17; W: 19 cm
OIM 10681

This object, traditionally called an aegis, was carried
by musicians, priests, and also frequently by the
goddess Bastet. It is a representation in metal of a
beaded menat necklace. The multiple flexible strands
of the menat are represented as a broad collar with
falcon terminals around the neck of a female deity,
most commonly Hathor but sometimes also Isis or
the feline-form goddesses Tefnut, Sekhmet, Menhit,
and Bastet. This example probably represents Hathor

6, back

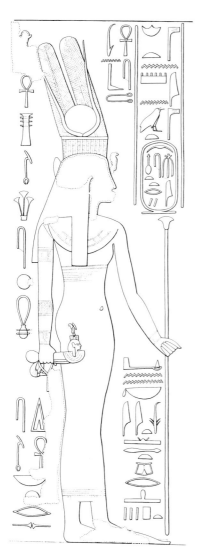

FIGURE 29. Queen Ahmose Nofertari holding a menat adorned with the head of the Goddess of Thebes. This form of menat counterpoise with a head appears to be the developmental link between the menat and the "aegis." Dynasty 21, ca. 1069 B.C. Epigraphic Survey, *Temple of Khonsu*, vol. 1, pl. 58

or Isis, both of whom wear the lyre-shaped headdress worn by the tiny seated goddess shown in the section of the broad collar below the goddess' chin.

The link between the flexible menat and the metal version can be seen in New Kingdom representations of a menat adorned with the head of a goddess (fig. 29). By the Twenty-second Dynasty, these two-dimensional images were translated into bronze objects. The back of this example has metal loops that allowed a bronze counterpoise (see cat. no. 7) to be hinged to it, just as a beaded collar would have a counterpoise. When carried, the aegis was held by the counterpoise, exposing the shield shape of the collar and the deity's face to the onlooker (see cat. no. 8). They were probably also used as offerings that were left in temples to show one's devotion to the gods.

The term "aegis," the Greek term for the shield of Zeus or Athena, is a long-standing misnomer for this type of object. A shield-shaped ornament, also called an aegis, is shown on the bow and stern of sacred boats used to transport the Egyptian gods and the king in procession (fig. 30). Those ornaments, which have the head of the deity, served to identify the occupant of the boat.   ET

FIGURE 30. The priest Khons offers incense and a libation to the boat of the god Khonsu. The identity of the god within the boat's veiled shrine is established by the aegises on the bow and stern which are ornamented with the falcon head of the god Khonsu. Tomb of Khons at Thebes (Theban Tomb 31), Dynasty 19, ca. 1250 B.C. Photo: C. F. Nims

7. MENAT COUNTERPOISE

Bronze
Third Intermediate–Late Period, Dynasties 22–31,
ca. 945–332 B.C.
Gift of Helen Swift Neilson, 1944
H: 15.0; W: 6.5 cm
OIM 17570

This object's form is derived from an ornament that was attached to a multi-strand necklace of beads called a menat (see figs. 25, 26, 31). The menat had a specifically protective function beyond its musical role, for temple reliefs show goddesses wearing a menat around their neck, extending the beaded necklace toward the nose of the king. The accompanying inscriptions refer to life and protection being granted by the act (fig. 31).

Menats are most commonly shown in the hands of queens, princesses, and female singer-priestesses. Among deities, Hathor, Mut, Sekhmet, and Tefnut are shown wearing them and, for unknown reasons, the menat was the characteristic emblem of the male god Khonsu.

The lobed counterpoise evolved from clasps that joined the multiple beaded strands of the necklace. It acted as a counterweight to keep the back of the necklace from digging into the wearer's neck. This example is decorated with heads of the lion-headed god Menhit topped with a sun disk and uraeus and Onuris with his feathered headdress with uraeus. Their heads emerge from a shared broad collar. Onuris and Menhit are associated with an episode of the Myth of the Eye of the Sun that recounts that the sun god's daughter, the Eye of the Sun, fled to Nubia where she transformed herself into a fierce lioness, shown here as Menhit. Onuris, who bore the epithet "He-Who-Brought-Back-the-Distant-One," was sent to retrieve the Eye and to make the Sun whole again.

The shank bears an image of the same two gods who jointly hold a tall *was* scepter, the symbol of dominion. The orb is decorated with an image of a carp with a papyrus stem in its mouth, swimming in a marsh. The carp was the cult symbol of Lepidotonopolis, a city north of Thebes that was the center of the worship of Menhit and Onuris.   ET

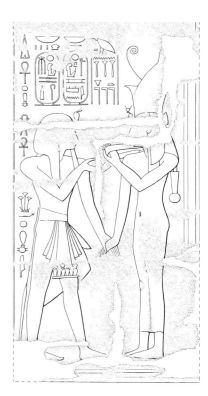

FIGURE 31. The goddess Mut extending her menat toward King Ramesses III. Karnak, temple of Ramesses III, Dynasty 20, ca. 1184–1153 B.C. Epigraphic Survey, *Reliefs and Inscriptions at Karnak*, vol. 1, pl. 51d

8. FIGURINE OF BASTET

Bronze
Late Period, Dynasty 26, 664–525 B.C.
Gift of the Art Institute of Chicago, 1917
H: 7.4 cm
OIM 9458

This small, solid-cast bronze figurine represents the cat-headed goddess Bastet. Bastet was routinely portrayed as a domestic cat or as a woman with a cat or a lion head adorned with a uraeus. Here she wears a tight-fitting sheath dress that reaches her ankles. She carries a sistrum, a ritual menat (see cat. nos. 4–5, 7), and a semicircular basket. Although now indistinct due to corrosion, her menat appears to have a head of Bastet or Sekhmet-Bastet, as is common on such statues. The function of the basket is unknown, although it has been suggested that it may have been for carrying kittens, the offspring of Bastet.

The association of Bastet with temple music is related to an episode of the Myth of the Eye of the Sun. This myth relates that Hathor, Mistress of Music, took the form of a feline (usually identified as Sekhmet) to attack mankind. Music appeased her and transformed her into the benign form of a cat. One ancient text concisely says: "When Hathor is angry, she is Sekhmet; when she is happy, she is Bastet."

A great number of these statuettes are known and most are quite small. Some bear dedication inscriptions such as "May Bastet give life," suggesting that they were votive offerings that were left in a temple of Bastet to demonstrate the donor's piety. Examples of these temples have been excavated at Bubastis, Saqqara, and elsewhere.   ET

(fig. 32). The curved neck and sound box are carved of a single piece of wood. The long narrow sound box would have been covered with skin that is now missing. A tapering piece of wood, called the hitch rail, is loosely socketed into the upper end of the sound box. One end of the gut strings was attached at the notches on the hitch rail, and the other was wrapped around the neck of the harp and secured by pegs. The vibration of the strings was transferred to the hitch rail and amplified by the sound box. This style and size of harp normally had four strings; other types had ten or more. The four pegs are ancient.   ET

9. HARP

Wood
New Kingdom–Late Period, Dynasties 18–26,
1400–525 B.C.
Luxor, Dra abu el Naga
By Exchange with the Metropolitan Museum of Art, 1958
L: 83; W (sound box): 8 cm
OIM 19474

Harps are rarely shown being played inside ancient Egyptian temples, but they are a prominent feature of religious festivals when the god left the temple and ventured out into the community. They are most commonly seen in reliefs in tombs where the tomb owner's wife is shown playing the harp for her husband or in banquet scenes where they are played by both men and women.

This harp would have been balanced on the shoulder and the strings plucked with both hands

FIGURE 32. Woman playing a harp. From the tomb of Nebamun (Theban Tomb 17), Dynasty 18, ca. 1400 B.C. Photo: C. F. Nims

10. RELIEF OF DANCERS AND SINGERS

Limestone
Old Kingdom, Dynasty 5, ca. 2504–2347 B.C.
Purchased in Cairo, 1920
H: 37; W: 28; Th: 5 cm
OIM 10590

Women were involved in ritual music and dance as early as the Old Kingdom. This fragment from an unidentified tomb shows two women and the hands of a third to the far left. The women on the left clap their hands to keep time to the music, while the woman on the right raises one hand and places the other on her hip as she dances. The women wear short, rounded hairstyles and tight-fitting dresses with wide shoulder straps and broad collar necklaces. The woman to the right also wears a sash tied at her hip. This ornament is characteristic garb for members of a group of professional musicians called the *khener* who were employed by the palace, temples, and funerary estates. Scenes of these performers are known from tombs as early as the Fourth Dynasty (ca. 2639 B.C.), where they dance in association with funerary offering rites or funerary processions.

In the New Kingdom, similar activities are shown in conjunction with festivals. In the tomb of Kheruef at Thebes, a line of women who are called "musicians who are singing and clapping at the time of the performance of the erection of the *djed* pillar" beat a small round drum and clap to the music (fig. 33). Behind them, women raise their hands above their head as they dance. The bands that cross their chests are associated with people of Libyan background, which is echoed in the caption which states that they are "women who have been brought from the oases" for the celebration of the ceremony.   ET

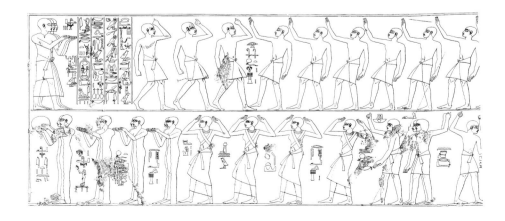

PUBLISHED

Vandier, *Manuel d'archéologie Égyptienne*, pl. 18, fig. 205 (left); Teeter, *Ancient Egypt*, no. 6.

FIGURE 33. Singers and dancers celebrate the jubilee festival of king Amunhotep III. From the tomb of Kheruef (Theban Tomb 192). Dynasty 18, ca. 1352 B.C. Epigraphic Survey, *Tomb of Kheruef*, pl. 59

RITUAL OBJECTS

Emily Teeter

In addition to playing music, priestesses participated in rituals that honored the king and the gods.

11. OFFERING TO THE GOD

Wood, gesso, pigment
Third Intermediate Period, Dynasty 22, ca. 946–735 B.C.
Luxor, the Ramesseum
Gift of the Egypt Exploration Fund, 1896
H: 25; W: 22 cm
OIM 1351

Priestesses performed many roles in the temple in addition to that of musician. This stela shows a woman named Djed-Khonsu-iw-es-Ankh ("Khonsu-Says-She-Will-Live"), before the seated god Re-Horakhty. She pours a liquid offering, probably cool water, from a slender vessel (see cat. no. 13) onto a table of offerings laden with round loaves of bread, a

Scenes, primarily from private tombs, show them using specific types of vessels in the course of rituals.

basket of dates(?), a bunch of grapes, a covered dish, two leeks, and a bouquet of flowers. Two containers called situlae (see cat. no. 12), that held milk or other liquid offerings, hang from the edges of the table.

The stela is contemporary with Meresamun and it gives a good idea of the appearance of an elite woman of that time (compare fig. 8). Djed-Khonsu-iw-es-Ankh wears an elaborate hairstyle (or wig) that covers her back and shoulders. Her wide pleated dress flows around her body, the voluminous fabric of the dress being an indication of her wealth. The dress is edged with green and red fringe that echoes the colors of her wide beaded collar. The artist may have allowed the woman's body to show through the dress to emphasize her femininity, or he may have been attempting to indicate that the linen was so fine that it was nearly transparent. In this era, women's bodies are shown in a more voluptuous manner, especially in contrast to the older tradition of an extremely slender ideal. Djed-Khonsu-iw-es-Ankh wears what is usually interpreted as a cone of scented fat on her head. It is decorated with a lotus and mandrake or persea fruit, both of which are evocative of sexuality and rebirth.

The brief text states that Djed-Khonsu-iw-es-Ankh was the daughter of a priest named Ser-Djhuty who served as Chief of the Mysteries of the Clothing for the Divine Cult Statue of Amun-Re. His titles indicate that he was responsible for the cloth in which the divine statue was garbed during the daily offering ritual. Considering the Theban provenance of the stela, it is very likely that Ser-Djhuty worked at the temple of Amun at Karnak, the same temple in which Meresamun may have served as a priestess-musician.   ET

PUBLISHED (SELECTED)

Lichtheim, "Situla No. 11395," p. 174, pl. 7A; Quibell, *The Ramesseum*, pp. 11, 17, pl. 20.4; Teeter, *Ancient Egypt*, no. 49; Wilson and Barghusen, *Highlights from the Collection*, no. 2.

12. RITUAL VESSEL (SITULA)

Copper alloy, pigment
Late Period, Dynasties 25–31, 747–332 B.C.
Purchased in Cairo, 1920
H (overall): 30.7; H (of vessel): 19.8; D (of rim): 5.7;
Maximum D: 13.9 cm
OIM 11394

Metal vessels with wire handles, called situlae, were used in temple rituals. Texts indicate that they held cool water or milk that was used in temple as well as in funerary rituals (cat. no. 11). Situlae have been recovered in considerable numbers from the ruins of the Late Period temple of Thoth at Saqqara. Some seem to have been used in rituals, while others are inscribed with pleas or prayers to the god Thoth to give health and life. These were probably offerings left at the temple in an effort to gain the god's favor.

This example was made for the funerary cult of a woman named Ta-baket-en-ese. The text on it, Spell 32 from the Book of the Dead, refers to the cool water that was poured from the situla onto an offering table to slake the thirst of the deceased. Ta-baket-en-ese's son Pen-maa, dressed as a funerary priest, with a leopard skin cloak, is shown pouring water from a *hes* vase (cat. no. 13) onto an offering table (in the form of the hieroglyph for "offerings"). He holds an elaborate incense burner in his other hand.   ET

PUBLISHED

Teeter, *Ancient Egypt*, no. 50.

13. RITUAL VASE

Faience
New Kingdom, Dynasty 18, reign of Amunhotep II,
ca. 1425–1401 B.C.
Purchased in Egypt, 1920
H: 27.5; D: 8.5 cm
OIM 10578

FIGURE 34. Princesses holding electrum *hes* jars at the jubilee (Sed) ceremony of Amunhotep III. Pairs of larger vessels with conical lids are in stands behind the princesses. From the tomb of Kheruef (Theban Tomb 192). Dynasty 18, reign of Amunhotep III, ca. 1352 B.C. Drawing: Epigraphic Survey, *Tomb of Kheruef*, pl. 31

This type of jar was used in temple ceremonies and in rituals of purification. Its slender form imitates the hieroglyph "*hes*" which means "to praise"; therefore the act of pouring liquid from it served to honor the recipient of the ritual. Stelae and scenes from private tombs show *hes* jars being used by priestesses and ordinary women, as well as by the king and other members of the royal family (fig. 34). They are also carried by rows of gods who personify the natural wealth of the Nile Valley. Other temple scenes show deities using *hes* jars to symbolically pour life (shown as a shower of small ankh signs, ☥) over the king as a sort of purification. The vessels were also carried by the king during a ritual dance that he performed at the jubilee ceremony that marked the thirtieth anniversary of his rule. *Hes* jars probably contained water or wine. Most scenes showing them are captioned generically "a liquid offering."

The captions for some *hes* scenes mention that the jars were made of precious metal, most often gold or electrum, and that they were a part of the temple treasury. A solid gold example, 19.5 cm tall, was recovered from the tomb of King Amenemope at Tanis.

This example is of faience. It bears a brief inscription, "the good god, Aa-kheperu-Re [Amunhotep II], beloved of Osiris." It is a non-functional copy of a *hes*. The lack of the characteristic curving spout (fig. 34) and the reference to the king being beloved of Osiris (the main deity of the afterlife) suggest that it was made to be deposited in the tomb of Amunhotep II.   ET

14. RECORD OF DELIVERY OF PROVISIONS FROM TEMPLE

Limestone, pigment
New Kingdom, Dynasty 19, reign of Ramesses II,
ca. 1221 B.C.
Purchased in Egypt, 1925
H: 28.0; W: 20.5 cm
OIM 12296

Egyptian temples during and after the New Kingdom engaged in activities that surpassed their primary religious character and encompassed socioeconomic duties. That same principle applied to memorial temples dedicated to the royal cult on the Theban west bank, which on the occasion of certain festivals would disburse provisions to multiple segments of the population. As a presumed employee of the temple of Amun, Meresamun would have been aware of this role of the temples as both donors and recipients of food and other goods.

This text details a series of food deliveries originating from the memorial temple of Thutmose I (ca. 1504–1492 B.C.) in the fifty-eighth regnal year of Ramesses II (ca. 1221 B.C.). Although not explicit in the text, the intended recipients of these provisions may have been the workmen of the Deir el-Medina settlement, which was located less than two miles away from the temple of Thutmose I, whose cult and temple appear to have remained functioning 270 years after his death.

The delivery included a variety of food items in considerable quantities, such as different types of bread, grains, cuts of meat, vegetables, milk, and beer. These were carried from the temple in seven separate consignments by Pasur and Huy, two *medjay*, or policemen (the name derives from an ancient Nubian tribe, whose members became mercenaries for the Egyptians and formed the police corps in the Ramesside period).

The police force was originally established to ensure the protection of the royal necropoleis of western Thebes. The *medjay* were not employed by any temple nor did they reside in the town of Deir el-Medina. Although the intricacies of their relationship with the inhabitants of that settlement remain unclear, there appears to have been very

frequent interaction between them and the workmen, both positive and otherwise. In fact, the *medjay* acted frequently as the only intermediaries between that restricted community and the outside, and this text could in fact highlight one such episode, whereby the *medjay* delivered a rich assortment of foodstuffs to Deir el-Medina, perhaps during or immediately following a festival.

This ostracon appears to have been re-used at a later time by a draftsperson who drew multiple figures of bees on the reverse side. Although breaks at the bottom and on the right and left sides have resulted in the loss of some of the text, the thirteen surviving lines preserve the greater part of the content.   HP

PUBLISHED

Transcription: Kitchen, *Ramesside Inscriptions*, vol. 7, pp. 188–89; Translation: Helck, *Die datieren und datierbaren Ostraka*, pp. 75–76.

ORACLES

Emily Teeter

Oracles, or pronouncements from the god, were an important part of life in ancient Egypt. The god normally dwelled in his or her sanctuary and was inaccessible. However, during festivals and certain other occasions, the god, represented by a statue, left the confines of the temple. The divine image was placed in a portable shrine that was loaded onto a ceremonial boat. The boat was then placed on a set of carrying poles supported on the shoulders of a double file of priests. As the procession moved from the temple into the community it was accompanied by temple musicians who shook their sistra and menats, and, in some cases, played flutes, drums, and other instruments.

Once outside the temple, people could approach the god and present their petitions. These were usually in the form of a yes or no question. The god gave his assent in several ways. Some texts refer to the sacred boat shaking or its bow dipping down as the god became "heavy." Others recount that the boat moved toward the question, which meant "yes," or backed away, which meant "no." Other oracles apparently gave spoken judgments.

Oracles became very common in Egypt in the first millennium B.C., and they are especially well documented in Thebes. Oracles were commonly consulted in disputes about property and inheritance, especially when local courts were unable to resolve the matter.

The community's reliance upon oracular decisions and the seemingly casual relationship between men and their gods is reflected by a letter dating to about 1070 B.C., in which a man literally ordered the god to make an appearance:

> When I was looking for you [the god] to tell you some affairs of mine, you happened to be concealed in your sanctuary.... See, you must discard seclusion today and come out in procession in order that you may decide upon the issues involving seven kilts belonging to the temple of Horemheb and also those two kilts belonging to the necropolis scribe....[1]

NOTE

[1] Wente, *Letters*, p. 219.

15. ORACLE STATUE

Serpentine (metal beak is modern restoration)
Late Period, Dynasties 25–31, 747–332 B.C.
Purchased in Cairo, 1919
H: 59.6; W: (breast) 23.4; Th: (base) 55.9 cm
OIM 10504

Some oracle statues gave judgments by motion, others gave vocal pronouncements. This oracle statue of a falcon probably represents the god Horus. Its use as an oracle is suggested by the hole that was drilled from the top of the bird's head through the body to the tail. Another interior channel runs from the top of the head to the beak. The channel probably allowed for the voice of a priest speaking on behalf of the god to be transmitted from behind a partition.

Other oracles are known to have given auditory signals. A statue of the falcon god Re-Horakhty and one of the deified queen Arsinoe (third century B.C.) were bored out in a similar manner as this falcon. The base for a statue of a bull excavated at Kom el-Wist (near Alexandria) was once connected to a bronze "speaking tube" that was thought to relay the voice of a priest to the petitioner. Similar ways of allowing unseen priests to become involved in oracles have been noted at temples at Karanis, Kom Ombo, and Dendur.   ET

PUBLISHED

Von Bothmer, "Nodding Falcon"; Marfoe, *Guide*, p. 23, fig. 11; Teeter, *Ancient Egypt*, no. 48; Wilson and Barghusen, *Highlights from the Collection*, no. 14.

Hieroglyphic transcription of the hieratic text

16. ORACULAR INQUIRY

Fragment of a baked clay vessel, pigment
New Kingdom, Dynasty 20(?), ca. 1186–1069 B.C.
Purchased in Egypt, 1939
H: 5.5; W: 7.0 cm
OIM 18876

Oracular requests represent an important component of the belief system of ancient societies. The earliest written evidence for this practice in Egypt dates to the New Kingdom, though divine consultation surely existed earlier.

This concise two-line oracular query possibly dates to the Twentieth Dynasty and probably originates from the workmen's settlement of Deir el-Medina. An oracular question such as the one conveyed by this text would be directed to the statue of a deity, which acted as the god's double. It is likely that this particular question was addressed to the deified king Amunhotep I (ca. 1525–1504 B.C.), whom the inhabitants of the west bank of Thebes consulted in oracles more often than other gods during the New Kingdom. Such inquiries would usually be presented during one of many annual festivals, and this text may have been drawn up on such an occasion, though the request may also have been submitted to the god at any other time, given the preponderance of chapels dedicated to Amunhotep I on the Theban west bank.

As illiteracy was widespread in antiquity, a trained scribe had to be commissioned to compose this request, which was presented by an anonymous person and contains a bipartite question. It inquires whether the individual should bring (or hire?) a woman by the name of Tabaket[1] and, secondly, whether she would become beneficial for him.

TRANSLATION OF THE HIERATIC TEXT:

Should I bring (hire?) Tabaket (or "the maidservant")? Will she become (effective) (with me)?

Such questions are intended to elicit a "yes" or "no" answer from the god, but it is difficult to determine what the divine response was to the present query, as the outcome of the request was perhaps deemed unnecessary to record, once the supplicant received an answer from the deity.   HP

NOTE

[1] An alternative to the personal name would be the noun phrase "the maidservant."

PUBLISHED

Černý, "Troisième série," p. 68, no. 95, and pl. 25, no. 95 (without transliteration or translation).

ANIMAL CULTS AND ANIMAL MUMMIES

Elise V. MacArthur

There is evidence of animal cults as early as the Predynastic period, but their popularity increased dramatically beginning in the Late Period (747–332 B.C.). Unfortunately, the reason for this increase in interest is unclear. Some scholars have attributed their popularity to the influx of foreign populations in Egypt in the Late Period, relating the cults to foreign religious practices. However, one inscription specifically mentions that the ibis catacombs at Athribis were hidden from foreigners (probably referring to the Persians), suggesting that animal cults were an Egyptian custom. Other scholars have suggested that the Egyptians might have viewed the foreign invasions of the Late Period as a sign of the gods' dissatisfaction, and the animal cults were an attempt to appease the deities. Regardless of the impetus, the popularity of animal cults continued to increase until the Edict of Theodosius (A.D. 379) outlawed the burial of animals along with other pagan practices.

Virtually all species of animals had divine associations, for example, cats with Bastet, crocodiles with Sobek, ibises with Thoth, and serpents with Apophis. Animals associated with the resident deity were raised in that god's temple. The production of animal mummies was an important part of the priests' duties. Initially, they raised the animals, and then at their natural or ritually scheduled deaths, the animals were embalmed. Priests prepared mummies of various qualities and prices, including plainly or elaborately wrapped animals (figs. 35–36), examples decorated with molded linen, and mummies enclosed within pottery or bronze coffins (cat. nos. 19–20, fig. 39). Pilgrims purchased the mummies from the priests, then donated them back to the temple of the specific god. Periodically, the priests would place the mummies in the temple's catacomb (fig. 37).

Priests also produced fake mummies. It is not clear whether this was a response to the lack of enough "real" animals to satisfy the demand of pilgrims or simply a shortcut. In either case, the practice does not seem to have been officially sanctioned, as indicated by texts from the archive of Hor, a priest who worked in the ibis catacomb. These texts record the punishment of priests who prepared fake ibis mummies and the declaration of the rule of "one god in one vessel," which stipulated that there must be one ibis (and not just parts) in each jar in the catacomb.

Another type of animal cult was centered on live animals that were believed to be the living representative of the god. Examples include the Apis, Buchis, and Mnevis bulls, crocodiles at Thebes and the Faiyum (which, according to Herodotus, were adorned with bracelets and earrings[1]), and the sacred falcons that dwelled in temples at Edfu, Athribis, and elsewhere.

Meresamun's potential involvement in animal cults is speculative, but references to the title "Maidservant of the Ibises"[2] suggest that some women worked in those institutions. Another text from the archive of Hor refers specifically to two women who seem to have functioned as diviners who interpreted an ibis oracle for the priests.[3]

NOTES

[1] Herodotus, *The Histories* II.69.

[2] "May Thoth the Ibis, the great god, give life to the children of the Maidservant of the Ibises." Martin, *Tomb of Hetepka*, p. 58.

[3] Ray, *Archive of Hor*, p. 61, "preliminary remarks" to no. 15.

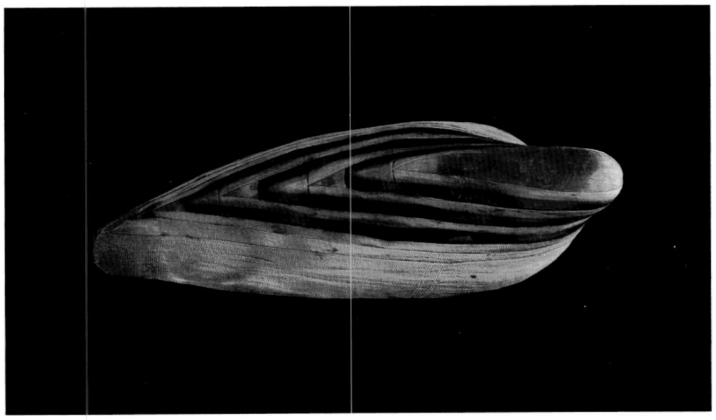

FIGURE 35. Mummified ibis. From Abydos. Roman period. OIM 9238

FIGURE 36. Mummified cat. Roman period. Museum August Kestner no. 2903. Courtesy of the Museum August Kestner, Hanover

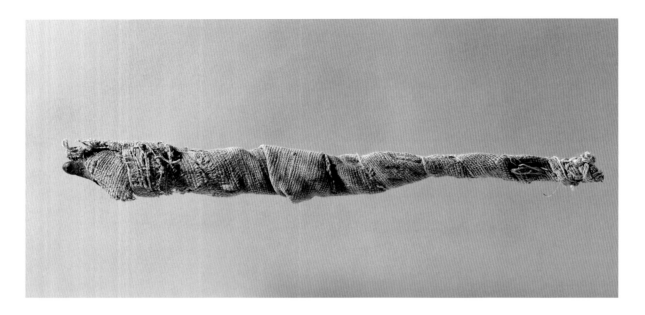

17. MUMMIFIED CROCODILE

Organic remains, linen
Late Period, Dynasties 25-31, 747-332 B.C.
Purchased in Shegilgil, 1894-1895
L: 29.4; W: 2.5 cm
OIM 701

According to Herodotus, there were cults dedicated to the god Sobek in Thebes and the Faiyum. In these temples, crocodiles were tamed and well treated. For example, at Medinet Madi in the Faiyum, archaeologists discovered a crocodile nursery that had an incubation area for eggs and a shallow basin of water in which baby crocodiles could swim. Adult crocodiles, moreover, were adorned with jewelry and given special offerings of food. They died either a natural or a premeditated death: some crocodiles were sacrificed at a young age to be votive offerings; others died of natural causes. Regardless, they were embalmed and interred in the temples' sacred catacombs upon their deaths. Mummified infant crocodiles, such as this example, have been discovered in the mouths of adult crocodile mummies, probably reflecting the means by which mother crocodiles have been known to transport their young in order to ensure their safety. EVM

18. MUMMIFIED IBIS

Organic remains, linen
Ptolemaic period, 332–30 B.C.
Abydos, Ibis Cemetery
Excavated by the Egypt Exploration Fund, 1913–1914
L: 31.5 cm
OIM 9237

Birds were mummified whole, often with their heads and beaks tucked down between their shoulders, or with their heads set up high and their beaks brought down between their wings. They were also mummified in part, as a package containing wings bound together with linen. These mummies or mummy bundles were interred with eggs in tall storage jars, which were then deposited in catacombs associated with the temple. Ibises, in particular, were associated with the god Thoth. His sacred necropolis (the Ibiotapheion) at North Saqqara is believed to have housed over four million birds (fig. 37).[1]

The underside of the mummy bears a long fabric patch, which probably served to disguise an untidy junction of the strips.   EVM

NOTE

[1] Ray, *Archive of Ḥor*, p. 138.

18, front

FIGURE 37. View of the ibis catacomb at North Saqqara, showing the rock-cut structure with rooms stacked with pottery coffins of mummified birds. Courtesy of the Egypt Exploration Society, London

18, back

19. BRONZE CAT STATUETTE

Bronze, hollow-cast
Late Period, Dynasties 25–31, 747–332 B.C.
Purchased in Cairo, 1920
H: 27; L: 16; W: 7 cm
OIM 11390

A seated cat was a common representation of the goddess Bastet. As a domesticated animal, she embodied notions of sexuality and fertility. Women are known to have held positions in her temples. For example, a Nineteenth Dynasty stela found in the sacred animal necropolis at North Saqqara belonged to a singer of Bastet.[1]

This statuette was a sheath-like coffin for a mummified cat which would have been interred within the lower part of the figurine. Such objects were made using the lost-wax process, and the tangs (metal stubs on the underside of the statuette) that remain from the casting process allowed the statuette to be secured to a base — probably of wood. Hollow bronze headpieces (called "masks") were also used to adorn cat mummies (fig. 38).

At temples dedicated to the goddess, sacred cats were raised as votive offerings. Although these animals were generally well treated, they were killed at either ten months or two years of age in order to control their numbers without inhibiting reproduction.[2] After their death, they were mummified and interred in the Bubastieion (cat necropolis) at Saqqara. Some cats were mummified plainly and placed in statuettes; others were wrapped more elaborately, featuring geometric patterns (fig. 36) and life-like heads made of molded linen.

Similar statuettes bear incised or embossed decoration in the bronze and were also adorned with gold jewelry. The Oriental Institute statuette bears an incised winged scarab beetle pectoral on its chest. Such pectorals (see cat. no. 57) magically protected wearers. The winged scarab beetle was associated with notions of rebirth. **EVM**

FIGURE 38. Cat mask. Late Period, Dynasties 26–31, 664–332 B.C. OIM 18826

NOTES

[1] Martin, *Tomb of Hetepka*, p. 42, no. 130.
[2] Armitage and Clutton-Brock, "Radiological and Histological Investigation."

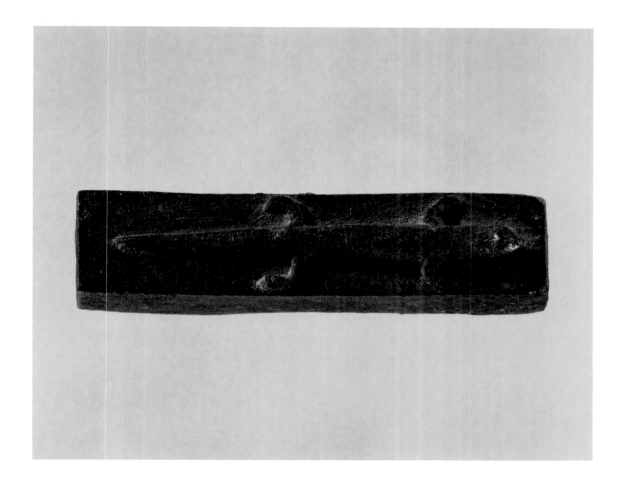

20. COFFIN FOR LIZARD

Bronze
Late Period, Dynasties 25–31, 747–332 B.C.
Gift of Virginia Lutzenkirchen, 1979
L: 12.3; H: 2.5; W: 3.0 cm
OIM 25605

Animal mummification gained popularity in the Late Period (747–332 B.C.). At this time, mummification included even small creatures, such as snakes, shrews, and scarab beetles. Some animals were buried in coffins made of metal, wood, or clay. The mummified remains of small animals, in particular, were often placed in bronze coffins, their likeness rendered in bronze on the lid of the coffin. This example once contained a mummified lizard. The coffin has corroded shut, but remnants of the lizard still rattle around inside. Another bronze coffin (fig. 39), once enclosed a serpent; it is depicted in a recoiled position on the lid of the coffin. EVM

FIGURE 39. Serpent coffin. Late Period–Ptolemaic period, 6th–1st centuries B.C. OIM 11189

MERESAMUN'S LIFE OUTSIDE THE TEMPLE

EMILY TEETER

There is rich documentation for the life of an ancient Egyptian woman like Meresamun. Scenes in tombs show the daily activities within elite households. Examples of clothing, furniture, jewelry, and ceramic vessels have survived, as have written records. Yet, unfortunately, our information relates to only a small portion of the population who had the resources to have a decorated tomb or rich home furnishings that survive until today. The much larger section of the population, the non-elite, is not well represented by detailed records of their own activities, partially because archaeologists have yet to focus on studying non-elite settlements. However, their lives can be documented secondarily through the artistic and textual sources left by those who may have employed them in their houses or on their farms (fig. 40).

By virtue of their social and legal rights, ancient Egyptian women had opportunities for a wider range of activities than many of their contemporaries in the ancient world, yet the sphere of primary activity for ancient Egyptian women was the home or the home-estate (see cat. nos. 71–72). A woman's most important responsibilities were to run the household, to raise her children, and to support her husband. Depending upon the economic resources of the family, this could be a very large and complicated undertaking, for the "mistress of the house" would have been responsible for coordinating and supervising house servants, bakers, brewers, weavers, and presumably for receiving and accounting for supplies from outside the confines of the house.

Overall, the pattern of life from birth through adolescence, marriage, the establishment of a household of her own old age, and ultimately, death, for a woman in ancient Egypt is very familiar to us today.

FAMILY, HOUSEHOLDS, AND MARRIAGE

From the surviving evidence, it appears that most Egyptian households in the time of Meresamun were, at least ideally, based on the immediate, nuclear family. Census lists from Thebes written several centuries before her time[1] show that houses in western Thebes were not occupied by extended families as is often the case in the modern Middle East. Ideally, upon marriage the couple moved to their own residence and lived there with whatever servants they could afford. However, there were variations in this pattern. Several stelae, most from the Middle Kingdom — long before the time of Meresamun — (fig. 41), show what appear to be the residents of a single household which includes the man, his wife, and their children with two half-sisters ("his sister of his mother") and the household staff, including a baker with his wife, mother, and daughter, and the family brewer with his sister. It is very likely that a man and wife would take in widowed siblings or aged aunts and uncles.

The non-royal population was monogamous. Although the genealogical records of Meresamun have not survived, there is no reason to assume that she was not married. Priestess-singers were not cloistered like Christian nuns. The genealogies of a few temple singers specifically state that they were the children of other temple singers, indicating that serving in the temple did not prevent women from marrying and having children.[2] Although there continue to be assertions that

FIGURE 40. Unnamed servants shown on the estate of Minnakht at Thebes. Two men present incense (*top register*), porters carry a large chest (*middle*), and a butcher prepares funerary offerings (*bottom*). Tomb of Minnakht, (Theban Tomb 87), Dynasty 18, ca. 1450 B.C. Photo: C. F. Nims

FIGURE 41. Stela showing the extended family of Senbu, including his half-sisters and house staff. From Abydos. Middle Kingdom, Late Dynasty 12-early Dynasty 13, ca. 1794-1648 B.C. OIM 6739

Considering that most people in ancient Egypt did not travel far from their villages, it is likely that most marriage partners were selected from the local population. It is not surprising that the Instructions of 'Onchsheshonqy contain the advice: "Do not let your son marry a woman from another town lest he be taken from you," advising parents to keep an eye on potential partners, and to keep their children, who would be their helpmates in later life, close to them.

Although we can only infer, it seems likely that marriages were to some extent engineered by parents who wished to make the most advantageous match for their children. In the Tale of the Doomed Prince (from late Dynasty 18) we read of a strong-willed daughter who opposed her father's choice of the man to be her husband. In the tale, the prince of Nahrin (Syria) endeavored to have his only child, a daughter, be courted exclusively by local princes. When an Egyptian prince, masquerading as a lowly chariot warrior's son, won the princess' heart, her angry father commanded, "Send him away!" The daughter defied her father, swearing to neither eat nor drink and to kill herself unless she was allowed to marry the Egyptian. Indeed, she got her way, and they were allowed to wed. The theme of romantic love is echoed in poetry, but it is not clear to what extent people could actually select their own marriage partners.

There does not seem to have been a pattern of marriage between cousins such as is prevalent in modern Egypt. Genealogies of eleven couples at Deir el-Medina (eleventh century B.C.) for whom the name of the parents of the spouses are given show no marriage between cousins. But there may have been considerable variation, for another group of households in Thebes in the Eighteenth Dynasty (fourteenth century B.C.) taken from genealogies in ninety-three tombs indicate that perhaps ten couples were indeed first cousins.[4]

Once established in a household, the community considered the couple to be "married." Although there did not seem to be societal prohibitions against pre-martial sex, once the household was established, fidelity was expected and even enforced by the community. In one of the clearest illustrations of the neighborhood enforcing societal norms, a text from the late Twentieth Dynasty (ca. 1070 B.C.) relates that a woman was engaged in an affair with a married man. After eight months, the community made their displeasure known and a group of the villagers went to beat the woman whose behavior was bringing shame on the

priestesses, especially the highest level — the God's Wives — were "virgin wives" of the god,[3] no direct evidence supports this assertion.

By today's standards, people were young at the time of marriage, and probably most girls were married about the time they reached puberty. Literary texts give some indication of the ideal age for marriage. The Middle Kingdom Instructions of Ptahhotep (ca. 2000 B.C.) counsels men to settle down "when you are capable," which may refer to the economic capability of establishing a household. The Instructions of (a man named) Any, composed in about 1200 B.C., suggests that a man marry when he is "young," while the Instructions of 'Onchsheshonqy (fifth century B.C., but probably composed in the Third Intermediate Period) recommends age twenty as the ideal age for a man to marry.

neighborhood, but a local official restrained them. The official warned the man to correct his behavior, saying that he would not prevent a beating if their relationship continued.[5]

Marriage was at least ideally seen as a loving and supportive relationship. In a letter from the New Kingdom, the duties of a man to his wife are stated as fidelity, (loving) attention, to care for her and their children, to care for his wife in sickness, "to take pride in her," and not to treat her as a master treats a servant.[6] There are many records that attest to happy and supportive marriages. In a Nineteenth Dynasty letter, a man recalls he remained married to his first wife as he climbed the career ladder from jobs instructing officers of the infantry and chariotry to the "post in which I am now": "I took you for a wife when I was a youth, and I functioned in every important office of pharaoh without divorcing (you)."[7] Marriage also provided arrangements for the division and control of wealth in the family and it protected the wife and her children if widowed or divorced (see the essay *The Social, Economic, and Legal Status of Women*, below).

Divorce was not uncommon and there are many examples of divorced people remarrying. Most divorces seem to have been initiated by the husband, but that may be a function of men's higher literacy rate and public presence. Although it is not entirely clear, it appears that women had the right to initiate divorce from about 500 B.C., and perhaps hundreds of years earlier. Grounds for dissolution of marriage include adultery, infertility, and simple incompatibility. However, divorce was not casual, and especially with the financial repercussions, one can assume that there was pressure from the couples' families to reconcile. Divorce could be formalized by swearing an oath in the local court confirming the dissolution of the marriage. Lists of divorces are also known. They may have been compiled to acknowledge and document the resulting division of property.[8]

As in all cultures, a major objective of marriage was the birth of children. In a culture with an emphasis upon procreation and fertility, the birth of a live and healthy child was the cause for great joy. Children were also seen as long-term insurance policies, for a child's major obligation was the care of elderly parents and to give them a proper burial and funerary rites. If a couple could not conceive, they could adopt.

During the era of Meresamun, the most common title associated with women is *nbt pr* "mistress of the house." The mistress of the house was responsible for maintaining the household, whether big or small. In a more modest house, a woman's day would be consumed with the endless chores of baking, brewing, cleaning, and doing laundry. In a more elite household, such as that of Meresamun, the woman would have taken a more supervisory role. Innumerable scenes show activities in elite households, but in most of the scenes, the wife is shown in a secondary role to her husband. It is the man who is shown watching over the farm hands, the craftsmen, and the household workers (fig. 49).

CHILDHOOD AND EDUCATION

Paintings, reliefs, and artifacts tell us something about childhood in ancient Egypt. The lifestyle of a child depended upon the social and economic standing of the family. Scenes of children working in fields indicate that children of lower-status families were expected to contribute to the household through their own labor. Young girls are often shown as house servants and attending at banquets. Some children of more elite families are shown in immaculate pleated gowns with hair carefully coiffed, mimicking the appearance and behavior of their parents (fig. 42).

Although there are many sources that document the formal education of boys, there is virtually no evidence for a similar program for girls. Ironically, a deity

FIGURE 42. Little girls, dressed in pleated linen dresses, imitate the appearance and decorum of their mothers at a banquet. Tomb of Sennedjem (Theban Tomb 1), Dynasty 19, ca. 1295–1186 B.C. Photo: C. F. Nims

associated with writing and record keeping is female: Seshat. The most irrefutable evidence for female literacy is administrative titles, such as *sesh-sehemet* "female scribe," but that occurs only in the Middle Kingdom, and whether it actually means a professional female scribe is debated. Other evidence for female literacy includes images of writing equipment under the chairs of elite women and a few examples of pen cases inscribed for women. There are references to schools that were attached to the palace, and perhaps princesses and girls of the most elite families received some tutoring in that institution.

The smattering of letters addressed from one woman to another are more difficult to interpret.[9] They could be indications of female literacy, or the texts could have been dictated by women to male scribes whose counterparts would read the letter to the recipient. Despite the difficulties with determining whether some elite women were literate, some must have been functionally literate for specific tasks, even if at a low level. For example, some women were merchants, which would necessitate at least the ability to read and issue receipts.

HOUSES AND HOMES

Houses were built of perishable mudbrick rather than of stone, and so they are very poorly preserved. Most of our evidence consists of clay or stone models, images of houses in tomb paintings, and a much smaller number of archaeological remains of houses themselves, usually just their foundations, which, unfortunately, do not give much information about the upper stories.

Urban houses were generally of two types, a sprawling estate (fig. 43) or a smaller, compact, city house (fig. 44). The latter would be typical of Meresamun's Thebes, because, during her lifetime, Thebes was among the largest cities in Egypt (the population has been estimated at 50,000), and space for houses would have been at a premium. A city house shown in the tomb of Nebamun (fig. 44) is two stories tall and has a decorative window and balcony above the door. As is typical of houses of this type, two wind scoops (known in Arabic as *mulqufs*) on the roof catch the fresh breeze and funnel it into the house.

A group of houses of the Third Intermediate Period, contemporary with Meresamun, was excavated by the Oriental Institute at Medinet Habu in western Thebes, a site with which she certainly would have been familiar. Like many Egyptian villages, it had haphazard city planning with narrow winding alleys dotted with garbage heaps. Houses shared a common wall with their neighbors (fig. 45). Smaller houses consisted of a wide front room and a larger central room (about 6.0 x 4.5 meters) often with one or two columns (fig. 46). Two areas, described as closets, were located behind the main room. Stairs led from the main room to the roof that probably served as a kitchen and warm-weather

FIGURE 43. The estate of Minnakht at Thebes. A walkway connects the house (*right*) to the lake. The house has a broad forecourt planted with two trees. Behind the main entry is a series of four rooms. Servants stand in the tree-filled fields that flank the house. Tomb of Minnakht, (Theban Tomb 87), Dynasty 18, ca. 1450 B.C. Photo: C. F. Nims

FIGURE 44. A small two-story townhouse. Two scoops on the roof funnel cool air into the home. Tomb of Nebamun (Theban Tomb 90), Dynasty 18, ca. 1390 B.C. Photo: C. F. Nims

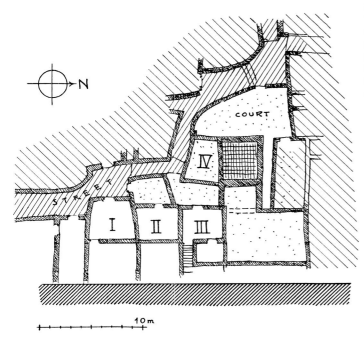

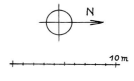

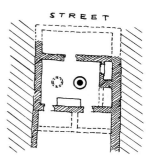

FIGURE 45. A group of houses in western Thebes. The houses are jammed together with shared walls. The lack of village planning is indicated by the meandering street onto which the houses open. Dynasties 22–24, ca. 945–715 B.C. Hölscher, *Excavation of Medinet Habu*, vol. 5, fig. 7

FIGURE 46. Plan of a small city house of the time of Meresamun. The central room has a pair of columns, probably of wood. Dynasties 22–24, ca. 945–715 B.C. Hölscher, *Excavation of Medinet Habu*, vol. 5, fig. 4

sleeping area. A small room under the staircase is often mentioned as being a space associated with women. Water was drawn from a nearby well. The houses have no indication of bathrooms, and so bathing may have been done with a bucket of water in the house, or in the Nile. The interior rooms of the houses would have been plastered and painted. The small size of these houses reflects the tradition of nuclear families, for none of them is large enough to accommodate multiple generations.

Meresamun's position as temple singer and the richness of her coffin suggest that she came from one of the elite families of Thebes, who, no doubt, would have lived in a more spacious house, perhaps situated in a walled garden with a stable for horses, silos, and a kitchen separated from the house itself. We have very little archaeological documentation of these more gracious homes at Karnak. One larger "villa," dating from a period slightly after her time, was excavated and documented.[10] Its entrance faced the temple, affording a grand view. The strong foundations suggest that it was several stories tall. Areas that could be identified include a large court and a kitchen with three ovens.

OLD AGE

Ideally, in old age a woman would be surrounded by her children and grandchildren. Egyptian texts stress respect for the aged and the obligation of the young to care for the old, and it is likely that a widow would live with her children. Texts express concern for the well-being of widows, for the normal social pattern was for a woman to be cared for by her husband. Even after the death of a husband, until she remarried, a woman was associated with her spouse as indicated by a reference to a woman as "the wife of Huy who is dead."[11]

Affection between spouses is well illustrated by the care that was given to the ill and by the grief shown at death. In a thirteenth-century B.C. letter written by a man to his deceased wife (a genre of literature called "letters to the dead") he recalls how he cared for his wife:

When you became ill with the disease that you contracted, I [sent for] a chief physician, and he treated you and did what you told him to do. Now when I went accompanying pharaoh in journeying south, this condition (death) befell you, and I spent several months without eating or drinking like a normal person. When I arrived in Memphis, I begged leave of pharaoh, and [came] to where you were. And I and my people [the family?] wept sorely for [you] .... I donated clothing of fine linen to wrap you up in and had clothes made. Now look, I've spent these last three years without entering (another) house [i.e., not having taken another wife], though it is not proper that one who is in the same situation as I be made to do this. Now look, I have done this out of consideration for you.[12]

Following an ancient Egyptian from birth through old age is a reminder of how little the basic human condition has changed over the millennia. The concern that parents show for their children, the affection shared by spouses, the desire for the basic comforts — a house of one's own, a job, security — are still as vital today as they were to Meresamun more than 2,800 years ago.

NOTES

[1] Kemp, *Ancient Egypt*, p. 307; Peet, *Great Tomb-Robberies*, pp. 83ff.

[2] Examples include Meresamunet, the daughter of Sheamenimes, and Tafabart, daughter of Tentmin. Ritner, "Fictive Adoptions," pp. 87, 89; Ritner, "Oblique Reference," pp. 351, 355.

[3] Yoyotte, "Divine Adoratrices," p. 182.

[4] Toivari-Viitala, *Women at Deir el-Medina*, p. 58.

[5] Janssen, "Marriage Problems"; Wente, *Letters*, p. 203.

[6] Johnson, "Mistress," p. 180.

[7] Wente, *Letters*, p. 216.

[8] Toivari-Viitala, *Women at Deir el-Medina*, pp. 93–94.

[9] Wente, *Letters*, pp. 174–75 (no. 290), pp. 200–01 (no. 38), and especially p. 181 (no. 297), where the author of the letter instructs the recipient to have a young girl "write a letter and send it to me."

[10] Redford, "East Karnak Excavations," pp. 77–79.

[11] Toivari-Viitala, *Women at Deir el-Medina*, p. 211.

[12] Wente, *Letters*, p. 217.

HOME FURNISHINGS

Pottery

Pottery was a ubiquitous part of any household. Plates, platters, large and small jars, cups, mugs, and pitchers were all made of baked clay. Unlike some other periods in Egyptian history, pottery from the time of Meresamun is generally undecorated. The favorite forms were open bowls (cat. no. 22) and wide-mouthed jars (cat. no. 23). In this era there was little difference in the style of pottery from region to region in the Nile Valley. As in other periods, imported pottery was used alongside that made in Egypt.   ET

21. BOWL

Baked clay
Third Intermediate Period, Dynasty 22, ca. 945–715 B.C.
Abydos, tomb D47
By Exchange with the Metropolitan Museum of Art, 1967
H: 4.6; D: 15.0 cm
OIM 26140

22. OPEN BOWL

Baked clay
Third Intermediate Period, Dynasty 23, ca. 818–715 B.C.
Abydos, tomb D99
By Exchange with the Metropolitan Museum of Art, 1967
H: 6.1; D (Rim): 24.1; D (Base): 7.7 cm
OIM 26141

23. JAR

Baked clay
New Kingdom–Third Intermediate Period,
Dynasties 18–25, ca. 1550–656 B.C.
Thebes, Khokha, tombs 827–835
By Exchange with the Metropolitan Museum of Art, 1967
H: 34.3; D: 41.9; D (Rim): 10.5 cm
OIM 29302

24. BOTTLE IN THE SHAPE OF A HEDGEHOG

Baked clay
Late Period, Dynasties 25–26, ca. 747–525 B.C.
Faiyum, grave F179
Egypt Exploration Fund excavations, 1901–1902
H:8.5; D: 7.2–6.2 cm
OIM 7182

Ceramic vessels with narrow openings like this one were used to hold small amounts of valuable oils or cosmetics. Compared to stone, baked clay was very malleable and could be molded into almost any shape with great detail. This vessel is shaped like a hedgehog. In ancient Egypt, the hedgehog was one of many animals associated with rebirth. This association was probably due to the fact that hedgehogs hibernate part of the year and live in underground burrows. Thus, these animals seemed to disappear into the earth and reemerge again alive and well, sometimes with baby hedgehogs! CDKJ

24,
back

Personal Grooming

Ancient Egyptian paintings feature scene after scene of beautifully coiffed and elaborately dressed men and women. Those scenes, along with a wide variety of grooming tools, cosmetics, and jewelry, indicate that the Egyptians cared passionately about their personal appearance. Hair was a particular obsession. Men, but also some women, generally kept their hair short, probably because it was cooler in the summer heat and easier to keep clean. But for special occasions, the elite of both genders wore elaborate wigs made of human hair or plant fiber. Hair or wigs could be decorated with fabric bands, beads, and rings of stone, faience, or metal.

Bodily cleanliness was also important, and texts indicate that the Egyptians bathed regularly. Although some texts and representations indicate that they removed all their body hair with tweezers, razors, or sticky poultices, clay figurines that represent pubic hair suggest that there was variation in practice.

Both men and women used makeup to protect and beautify the skin. Perfumed oils, generally made from animal fats and plant oils, scented the skin and also protected it from the dryness of the desert. Kohl, made of ground minerals (malachite or galena), enhanced the appearance of the eyes and may also have helped prevent bacterial eye infections. Most makeup was made of animal fat combined with a plant or mineral compound that could be ground and stored before being mixed and applied to the face.   CDKJ / ET

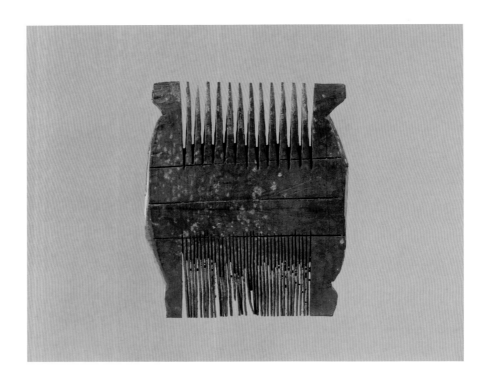

25. COMB

Wood
Greco-Roman period, 332 B.C.–A.D. 395
Faiyum
Gift of the Egypt Exploration Fund, 1901–1902
H: 8.5; W: 7.1; Th: 1.0 cm
OIM 7201

Combs were usually made from wood or ivory. They are often decorated with carved or painted designs. This example is relatively simple, the only design being the shaped sides, but the finely carved teeth show that it was an intricate piece of work nonetheless. The smaller teeth were helpful in removing pests like lice that could cling to the hair shaft.   CDKJ

26. MIRROR

Bronze, wood, gilt
New Kingdom(?), Dynasties 18–20, ca. 1550–1069 B.C.
Purchased in Egypt, 1933
H: 28.5; D (disk): 15.2 cm
OIM 16874

The ancient Egyptians were skilled at making glass jewelry and decorative bottles, but they did not use glass for mirrors. Instead, they employed disks of copper, or a copper alloy like bronze, that was polished to make a reflective surface. Over time, the metal oxidizes and corrodes so that extant examples of ancient mirrors no longer reflect at all.

The metal disks of hand mirrors have a tang of metal on their lower edge that allows them to be affixed to a handle. Some handles are carved with decoration that relates to feminine beauty — a figure of a slender girl, the face of Hathor who was the goddess of song, dance, music, and beauty, or, as this example, the drooping sepals of an open lotus blossom. The lotus blossom was associated with rebirth because the flower opened each morning in the warmth of the sun. This mirror symbolically replaced the rejuvenated flower blossom with the reflection of the viewer's face, alluding to her or his eternal rebirth. This may be part of an extended pun, for the word "mirror" in ancient Egyptian is the same as that for "life." The gold leaf on the handle of this mirror marks it as an especially luxurious item.   CDKJ / ET

PUBLISHED

Allen, *Handbook of the Egyptian Collection*, p. 109.

27. HAIR STYLING TOOL

Bronze
New Kingdom, Dynasties 18–19, ca. 1550–1186 B.C.
Gift of The Art Institute of Chicago
L: 7.9 cm
OIM 18185

In addition to combs, pincher-like tools were used to style hair. It is thought that one end of the rod was used to hold a small section of hair and twist it into curls or to tuck it into the elaborate styles seen on statues, reliefs, and paintings. Beeswax was used to help hold the hair in shape, the same way one might use hair gel today.   CDKJ

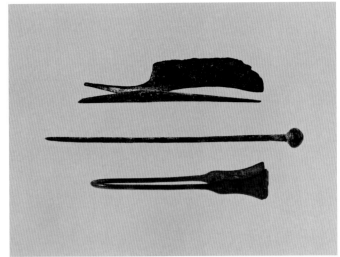

27
28
29

28. HAIR PIN

Copper alloy
Roman period, 30 B.C.–A.D. 395
Luxor, Deir el-Bahri
Gift of the Egypt Exploration Fund, 1904–1905
H: 11; D: 8 cm
OIM 8785

Pins like this one were used to hold elaborate hairstyles in place (fig. 47). They were often made of metal, but just as common were pins of carved wood, ivory, or bone. Pins were sometimes incised with decoration, painted, or shaped into decorative forms.   CDKJ

29. TWEEZERS

Copper alloy
Middle Kingdom, Dynasty 13, ca. 1773–1650 B.C.
Hu, grave Y501
Gift of the Egypt Exploration Fund, 1898–1899
L: 7.5 cm
OIM 5352

Ancient Egyptians groomed their body hair as well as the hair on their heads and, like today, tweezers were used to pluck stray hairs. This example is made of a single flexible piece of metal whose ends are in the form of lotus blossoms. Because lotus flowers (actually a type of water lily) close and drop below the water at night and rise and open every morning, they were associated with rebirth and rejuvenation. Personal grooming practices could rejuvenate one by giving one a more youthful appearance, and so lotus blossoms often adorned Egyptian cosmetic items.   CDKJ

FIGURE 47. Queen Neferu's hair being styled with the use of a pin like catalog no. 28. From the tomb of Queen Neferu, Deir el-Bahri, Dynasty 11, ca. 2008–1957 B.C. Charles Edwin Wilbour Fund, 54.49. Courtesy of The Brooklyn Museum

30. RAZOR

Bronze
New Kingdom–Late Period, Dynasties 18–31,
ca. 1550–332 B.C.
Luxor, Medinet Habu, tomb 12
Excavated by the Oriental Institute, 1930
H: 15.7; W: 12.0; Th: 5.1 cm
OIM 14426

The ancient Egyptians removed most of their body
hair as a part of cleanliness. Men who worked
in temples and participated in religious rituals
had to remove all their hair as part of their ritual
purification. Razors were made from copper or
bronze. They came in a several sizes and shapes,
probably so that they could be easily used on
different parts of the body. The curved end of this
example was the cutting edge. The razor was held
with two or three fingers curled around the stem-like
handle and the thumb braced on the point opposite
the blade.   CDKJ / ET

PUBLISHED

Hölscher, *Excavation of Medinet Habu*, vol. 5, p. 65 (9),
pl. 39b (21).

Jewelry

In most periods of Egyptian history, men and women
wore similar types of jewelry. Jewelry could be pure-
ly decorative, or it could afford the wearer amuletic
protection from harm. A wide range of materials was
used, including clay, semiprecious stones, and silver
and gold. However, the most common material is faience, a quartz-based material that was easily molded
or sculpted and was available in many colors.

Those who could not afford more valuable materials might have jewelry made of inexpensive materials,
such as baked clay or faience, in colors that would imitate the expensive stones such as carnelian, lapis lazuli,
feldspar, and jasper. The Egyptians seemed to prefer
stones that absorbed light rather than reflected it, and
so there is no tradition of using rubies, emeralds, dia-
monds, and other stones so valued in other cultures.

The Egyptians loved beads. They were made in a variety of materials, like clay and faience that could be molded into shape, or of stone that was carved and drilled. Beads were produced in many shapes, including rings, wide cylinders, long and narrow tubes, spheres, flat disks, and representational shapes like hieroglyphs, animals, and people. Often, a variety of different beads was strung on several intertwined strands in order to create decorative patterns.

Broad collars made of multiple rows of beads are omnipresent. They were worn by men and by women.

But necklaces and bracelets could be as simple as a string of identical beads, or very complex, made up of different sizes, shapes, and colors of beads and pendants on multiple strands of string or metal wire. The strings and wires that hold pieces of jewelry together break down over time so that beads are usually found scattered, making it difficult to recover the original stringing pattern. The jewelry shown here has been restrung to give an idea of what they might once have looked like. CDKJ / ET

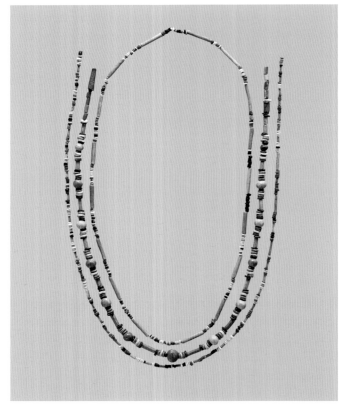

31 32 33

31. BEADS

Faience
Third Intermediate Period, Dynasties 21–25,
ca. 1069–656 B.C.
Gift of Charles Hitchcock, Chicago, 1906
L: 70 cm
OIM 8824a

32. BEADS

Faience
Middle Kingdom, Dynasties 11–12, ca. 2055–1773 B.C.
Hu, grave W23
Gift of the Egypt Exploration Fund excavation, 1898–1899
L: 64 cm
OIM 5524

33. BEADS

Faience
Third Intermediate Period, Dynasties 21–25,
ca. 1069–656 B.C.
Gift of Charles Hitchcock, Chicago, 1906
L: 77 cm
OIM 8824c

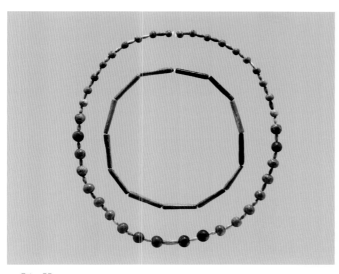

34   35

34. BALL AND BARREL BEADS

Faience
Middle Kingdom(?), Dynasties 11–12, ca. 2055–1773 B.C.
Egypt
Gift of Mr. Martin Ryerson, 1927
L: 78 cm
OIM 13665

35. TUBULAR BEADS

Faience
New Kingdom, Dynasties 18–20, ca. 1550–1069 B.C.
Egypt
Purchased in Paris, 1919
L: 52 cm
OIM 10427

36. BEADS WITH STONE COWRIE SHELLS

Faience, lapis lazuli, carnelian
Late Period, Dynasties 25–31, 747–332 B.C.
Luxor, Medinet Habu, tomb T10
Excavated by the Oriental Institute, 1931
L: 11.3 cm
OIM 15067

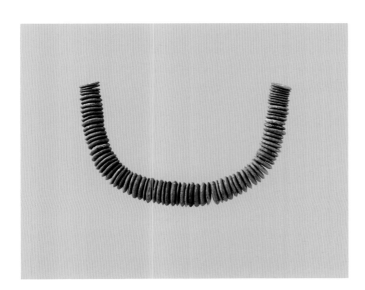

37. DISK BEADS

Faience
Late Period, Dynasty 25, 747–656 B.C.
Luxor, Medinet Habu, tomb T10
Excavated by the Oriental Institute, 1931
L: 23 cm
OIM 15082

Ear Spools

Ear spools were a type of earring that fit in a large hole in the earlobe. Most ancient Egyptians had pierced ears; after the initial piercing, the earlobes could be gradually stretched to accommodate an ear spool. Ear spools ranged in size and some, like the examples here, were quite large. They appeared first in the New Kingdom and continued to be popular at least through the Third Intermediate Period. Ear spools were worn by both men and women, and they could be made of a variety of materials including stone, glass, faience, and metal.   CDKJ / ET

Hair Rings

Hair rings were placed around strands or braids of hair in order to decorate the hairstyle. Several of them could be placed throughout the locks, creating points of color throughout one's hair. Like other pieces of jewelry, hair rings could be molded of clay or faience or carved of stone.   CDKJ

40   41   42

40. HAIR RING

Carnelian
Late Period, Dynasties 25–31, 747–332 B.C.
Luxor, Medinet Habu
Excavated by the Oriental Institute
D: 1.6 cm
OIM 15313

41. HAIR RING

Faience
Late Period, Dynasties 25–31, 747–332 B.C.
Luxor, Medinet Habu
Excavated by the Oriental Institute
D: 1.8 cm
OIM 15314

42. HAIR RING

Jasper
Late Period, Dynasties 25–31, 747–332 B.C.
Luxor, Medinet Habu
Excavated by the Oriental Institute
D: 2 cm
OIM 15315

38   39

38. EAR SPOOL

Calcite
Late New Kingdom–Third Intermediate Period(?),
Dynasties 19–25, ca. 1295–656 B.C.
Luxor, Medinet Habu
Excavated by the Oriental Institute
H: 2.4; D: 3.5 cm
OIM 14563

39. EAR SPOOL

Calcite
Late New Kingdom–Third Intermediate Period(?),
Dynasties 19–25, ca. 1295–656 B.C.
Luxor, Medinet Habu
Excavated by the Oriental Institute, 1929–1930
H: 2.4; D: 3.6 cm
OIM 15562

Cosmetic Jars

Small stone vessels like these were called "alabastra" (cat. nos. 43–45) after the Greek name for their characteristic cream-colored stone. They were used to hold valuable oils, ointments, and perfumes. Because one would usually have only a small amount of such expensive substances, a small container would suffice to hold it. The small opening of these vessels helped to keep the contents from evaporating.

Calcite ("Egyptian alabaster") was the most popular stone for cosmetic vessels. It was soft enough to carve easily but hard enough to not break easily. It also occurs in a variety of colors (white and yellow being by far the most common) that are banded with white. Calcite is so fine-grained that it can be polished to a shine and ground so thin that light shines through it.

Like alabastra, slightly larger stone vessels (cat. nos. 46–47), these small jars probably held cosmetic substances such as ointments, oils, or compounds for makeup. The fact that these vessels are larger and have wider openings suggests that their contents were less expensive and less likely to evaporate. It also indicates that the contents were used in greater quantity than perfume. Cosmetic compounds kept in these vessels could be scooped, spooned, or poured out. One of these vessels (cat. no. 46) clearly contained a liquid to be poured out because it has a spout.   CDKJ

43   44   45

43. COSMETIC JAR

Calcite
Greco-Roman period, 332 B.C.–A.D. 395
Purchased in Egypt, 1920
H: 12.4; D: 1.9 cm
OIM 11345

44. COSMETIC JAR

Calcite
New Kingdom(?), Dynasties 19–20, ca. 1295–1069 B.C.
Luxor, Medinet Habu
Excavated by the Oriental Institute, 1930
H: 5.2; D: 2.6 cm
OIM 14542

45. COSMETIC JAR

Calcite
New Kingdom–Late Period, Dynasties 18–31,
ca. 1550–332 B.C.
Purchased in Cairo, 1920
H: 10.4; D: 5.6 cm
OIM 11326

46. COSMETIC JAR

Calcite
Third Intermediate–Roman period(?),
11th centruy B.C.–4th century A.D.
Purchased in Cairo, 1920
H: 8.3; D: 10.0 cm
OIM 11316

47. COSMETIC JAR

Calcite
New Kingdom, Dynasty 18, ca. 1550–1295 B.C.
Purchased in Cairo, 1920
H: 13.6; D: 6.8
OIM 11321

HOUSEHOLD CULTS

Emily Teeter

Worship of the gods was not restricted to temples. They were also venerated in private houses by priests who were "off duty" and also by people who had no official connection with the temple. Some objects recovered from ruins of houses document these informal religious practices and beliefs such as petitions to the gods for assistance in having children, seeking health, or solving personal conflicts. Others are reminders of the Egyptians' belief that deceased ancestors or members of the community were active participants in daily life and were able to help or harm from the world beyond. Deities and spirits were generally considered to be approachable and ready to help the petitioner, but they could also be dangerous if they were not provided with offerings. These often simple objects, most made of affordable clay, record the deep piety of the Egyptians and their reliance upon religion for solving everyday problems, whether in a temple or at home.

48. EAR STELA

Limestone, pigment
Third Intermediate–Late Period, Dynasties 22–26,
ca. 945–525 B.C.
Luxor, Medinet Habu
Excavated by the Oriental Institute, 1929
H: 8.0; W; 5.7; Th: 2.1 cm
OIM 16718

People, whether priestesses or not, could worship their gods without going to a temple. This small stela is incised with five pairs of ears that represent a direct conduit to the god, much like an ancient mobile phone with a dedicated line to the deity. Although this example does not bear an inscription, other such stelae identify the ears as belonging to the god Ptah. These stelae demonstrate how accessible the gods were thought to be; they could be contacted any time, any place, and asked to intercede on any sort of problem.   ET

PUBLISHED

Teeter, "Animal Figurines," p. 195; Teeter, *Ancient Egypt*, no. 36; Brewer and Teeter, *Egypt and the Egyptians*, fig. 6.5.

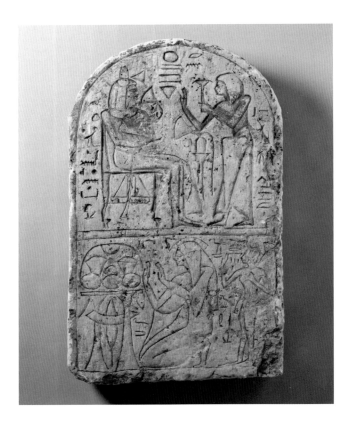

49. ANCESTOR CULT STELA

Limestone, pigment
New Kingdom, Dynasties 19–20, ca. 1295–1069 B.C.
Luxor, Medinet Habu
Excavated by the Oriental Institute, 1929
H: 36; W: 21; Th: 5 cm
OIM 14287

Religious ceremonies enacted in houses in the Theban area included the veneration of the spirits of deceased members of the family, called *akhs*. The Egyptians believed that these spirits stayed in contact with the world of the living. They could be contacted and, in return, they could initiate contact with the living. Members of the family would leave offerings before stelae such as this one as a means of keeping the *akh* happy and keeping an open line of communication. A satisfied *akh* could protect against a dizzying range of dangers: from the collapse of a wall, the fall of a thunderbolt, harsh words, or the bite of snakes and scorpions. But if it was not satisfied with offerings and prayers, there was a danger of it becoming a marauding spirit and causing difficulties for the living. *Akhs* lurked everywhere.

According to some texts, they lay in wait in pools, streams, wells, swamps, and even in heaven.

This stela relates to the cult of the "effective spirit (*akh*) of the god Re" (*akh iḳr n Rˁ*). This sort of spirit was thought have a special relationship with the sun god Re and to serve as an intermediary conveying people's prayers and requests to the god. About sixty examples of these stelae are known, most of them from the Theban area.

This stela commemorates a male *akh* named Nakht. Nakht is shown seated, sniffing a lily. His brother Sethmose, dressed in the distinctive kilt of a soldier, stands before him holding an incense burner. In the lower register, Nakht's sister Bakwerel and a young girl Tamit (whose relationship to Nakht is not stated) are shown. Bakwerel raises her hands in a gesture of prayer. As is typical with stelae of this sort, the dedicator was a close relative of the *akh*. The stela was recovered from the ruins of a private house at Medinet Habu.   ET

PUBLISHED

Demarée, *The ȝh iḳr n Rˁ-Stelae*, no. A26, pl. 7; Teeter, "Piety at Medinet Habu," p. 4, fig. 6.

50. VOTIVE FOOTPRINT

Baked clay
Late Period, Dynasty 25, 747–656 B.C.
Luxor, Medinet Habu
Excavated by the Oriental Institute
L: 9.8; W: 6.6; H: 3.3 cm (length of footprint from heel to
end of big toe: 8.5 cm)
OIM 14768

This lump of clay bears the impression of a child's
left foot. The edges of the toes have been detailed
with a sharp tool. It bears no inscription, and the
reverse is undecorated. This type of object is very
rare, but it presumably refers to the commemoration
of a birth or to the protection of a child.

It is possible that the imprint of the child's foot
was left in a household shrine or in the temple in
an effort to gain the god's protection or to thank
the deity for the birth. Although it is more usual

for statues to serve as an eternal substitute for the
individual, footprints alone had the same function.
Some graffiti of the outlines of feet on the roofs of
temples are captioned with texts that warn: "I will
erase the name of (i.e., symbolically kill) [him who]
destroys the footprints of [personal name]," equating
the permanence of the footprint with the individual's
lifespan. In a similar way, the impression of a child's
foot in clay would be a way of commemorating the
child and putting him or her under the protection
of the god. Such a dedication may be related to
theophoric names, such as Meresamun "Amun-Loves-
Her" or Djed-Khonsu-iw-ef-Ankh "Khonsu-Says-He-
Will-Live" that linked an individual and a patron
deity. This type of name became very common in the
Third Intermediate Period.   ET

PUBLISHED

Teeter, "Piety at Medinet Habu," p. 3, fig. 5; Teeter, *Baked
Clay Figurines*, no. 219.

51. VOTIVE BED

Baked clay, pigment
Third Intermediate Period, Dynasties 22–24,
ca. 945–715 B.C.
Luxor, Medinet Habu
Excavated by the Oriental Institute, 1929
H: 16.5; W: 24.0; Th: 1.5 cm
OIM 14776

Box-like clay models of beds, called votive beds, which have been recovered from houses as well as from temples, illustrate how some cult objects could be used in both contexts. The flat top of the votive bed is usually painted in imitation of webbing that supported the sleeper. The front section of the votive bed probably represents a scalloped-edged fabric covering. The decoration is flanked by figures of the god Bes, who was the protector of women and children. The figures represent the Bes-shaped legs of real beds depicted in tomb paintings and ostraca.

The front panel of this example is impressed with a scene of a nude woman standing in a duck-headed boat, her arms outstretched holding papyrus stems. Another woman stands on the stern. A plant motif — perhaps ivy, a symbol of rebirth — appears above the duck's head. The marsh setting of the scene refers to the ritual of plucking papyrus that was sacred to the goddess Hathor. The rustling sound of the papyrus in the swamp was equated with the sound of the sistrum and menat, both instruments associated with the worship of Hathor.

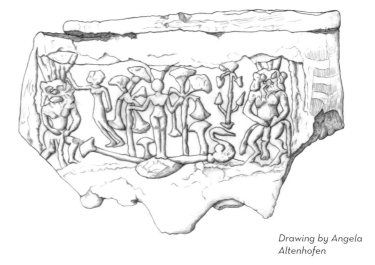

Drawing by Angela Altenhofen

Although the symbolism of the beds can be deciphered, their function in household and temple cults is not clear. They may have been small altars upon which figurines (see cat. nos. 52–54) were placed, or they may be models of larger architectural elements, called "birth beds," that also feature images of Bes. In either case, the Hathoric symbolism of their decoration and that fact that they are clearly little beds — an icon of the place of sexual union and birth — suggests that they are associated with regeneration. The large number of fragments of votive beds that have been recovered from houses and temples at Thebes attest to their popularity.   ET

PUBLISHED

Teeter, "Piety at Medinet Habu," p. 3, fig. 5; Teeter, *Baked Clay Figurines*, no. 236.

52   53   54

52-54. FEMALE FIGURINES

Baked clay, pigment
Third Intermediate Period, Dynasties 22-24,
ca. 945-715 B.C.
Luxor, Medinet Habu
Excavated by the Oriental Institute

52. OIM 14594; H: 10.5; W: 5.2; Th: 2.15 cm
53. OIM 14583: H: 12.6; W: 6.9; Th: 3.5 cm
54. OIM 14613; H: 8.8; W: 3.3; Th: 1.8 cm

Among the most common type of objects recovered from the ruins of houses, as well as from tombs and temples, are molded clay figurines of women. They appear in the Early Dynastic period and, with considerable stylistic development, they continued to be produced for more than 4,000 years, into the Islamic period. These examples, which are contemporary with Meresamun, represent an idealized slender woman. Catalog Nos. 52 and 53 show the woman on a bed, her hand to her breast to help her child suckle. On the larger example (cat. no. 53), the woman's hair is upswept on top of her head in a style associated with one who has recently given birth. The woman portrayed on Catalog No. 52 wears large spool earrings (see cat. nos. 38–39) that accentuate her sexuality and attractiveness.

Our understanding of the function of these figurines has progressed from the initial idea that they were "concubines" that would sexually entertain men in the afterlife to them being objects that allude not only to fertility and childbirth but also to a more generalized wish and desire for regeneration and rebirth without regard for gender. This new interpretation better explains why female figurines have been recovered from the tombs of women and children as well as men.   ET

PUBLISHED

Teeter, "Piety at Medinet Habu," p. 3, fig. 5; Teeter, *Baked Clay Figurines*, nos. 1, 27, 36.

Fertility and Birth Rituals

Elise V. MacArthur

Rituals that ensured fertility would have been important to Meresamun as a child and to any children she might have born. Childbirth was an extremely dangerous time for both women and newborn children. It has been estimated that 20 percent of pregnancies failed, 20 percent of all infants died within the first year of life, and 30 percent of the survivors did not live past age five.[1] As a result, a complex system of beliefs was founded on notions of fertility and protection. Various medical papyri (e.g., papyri Kahun, Berlin, and Carlsberg) describe tests one could perform in order to determine fertility, pregnancy, or the sex of the unborn child. One example deals with sickly newborns and their chances for survival: Papyrus Ebers (838) states, "If, on the day the child is born, it says 'ny' it will live and if it says 'mebi' it will die."

Certain deities were commonly associated with childbirth, such as Bes, Heqet, and Taweret. Their powers were invoked by means of magical objects — amulets, anthropomorphic vessels, and knives. These objects soothed both emotional and physical unease. Amulets and magic wands, in particular, would have been a source of comfort for expectant or potential mothers and for their young children. The salve once contained in certain anthropomorphic vessels was believed to relieve the bodily strains of pregnancy, which resulted in unsightly stretch marks and even miscarriage — a lingering danger for pregnant women.

It is understandable, then, that the role of mothers, and their contribution to society, was not taken lightly. A section from the Instructions of Any reflects upon the burdens with which mothers dealt to bring their children safely into adulthood: "Repay your mother for all her care. Give her as much bread as she needs, and carry her as she carried you, for you were a heavy burden to her. When you were finally born, she still carried you on her neck and for three years she suckled you and kept you clean." Indeed, Meresamun, as both child and mother, would have been closely connected to fertility magic.

NOTE

[1] Robins, "Women and Children," pp. 27–28. The burial of women with fully developed fetuses allows scholars to appreciate the risk of childbirth — for instance, Queen Mutnedjmet (wife of Horemheb), whose pelvic bones showed signs of a number of deliveries, was buried with her newborn child; Martin, *Lost Tombs*, p. 97; Strouhal, "Queen Mutnodjmet," p. 320.

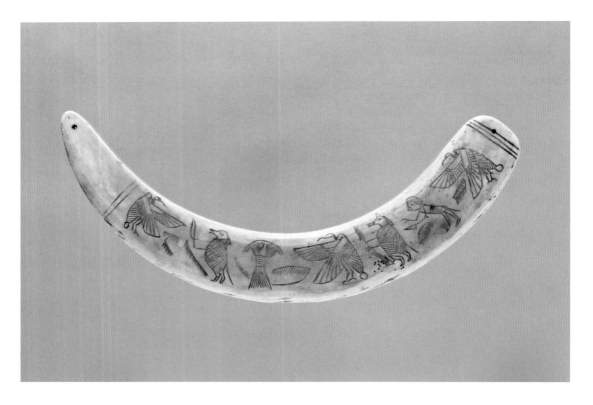

55. MAGIC KNIFE

Ivory
Middle Kingdom, Dynasty 12, ca. 1985–1773 B.C.
Purchased in Luxor, 1920
L: 23.1; H: 3.6; Th: 1.0 cm
OIM 10788

In the Middle Kingdom and Second Intermediate Period, apotropaic knives were used in rituals of magical protection for women and children of all social classes.[1] These knives, also referred to as "wands," were usually carved of hippopotamus ivory, invoking the protective powers of the hippopotamus goddess Taweret, who was closely associated with childbirth. Examples also exist in wood, faience, and calcite.

The decoration of each knife is unique, but it generally includes deities associated with childbirth. The Oriental Institute example features the goddesses Nekhbet and Taweret and the god Aha wielding knives, and a protective amulet (the hieroglyphic sign *s3*). Indeed, Nekhbet, a vulture goddess, is evocative of the hieroglyph for the word "mother" (*mw.t*). In addition, Aha (the "fighter"), like Taweret, was a deity associated with childbirth. He became the leonine dwarf god Bes in later periods. Some knives include inscriptions, which offered explicit protection for women and children: for example, "We [the gods] have come to protect the lady," and "We have come that we may extend our protection around the healthy child."[2]

The Oriental Institute knife bears two perforations, one at each end. Some examples have been found with a cord still running through such perforations, which scholars believe was used to carry or manipulate the objects. Other knives were discovered still wrapped in linen.

Based on wear patterns exhibited by the knives, it has been suggested that they may have been used to draw magical circles of protection on the ground around the beds of infants.[3] Some wands show signs of repair, implying a fair amount of use. After their use in life, these objects were deposited in burials, offering magical protection for the deceased during the process of rebirth. EVM

NOTES

[1] See examples in Altenmüller, "Ein Zaubermesser."
[2] Pinch, *Magic in Ancient Egypt*, p. 42; J. Allen, *Art of Medicine*, p. 29.
[3] Ritner, "Magical Wand," pp. 234–35.

56. PREGNANCY OINTMENT JAR

Calcite
New Kingdom, Dynasty 18, ca. 1550–1295 B.C.
Purchased in Cairo, 1920
H: 16.9; D: 6.0–7.9 cm
OIM 11313

Pregnant women were not often depicted in sculpture and relief. Instead, the idealized, slender female form was prominently featured. Among the exceptions, however, is a small corpus of Eighteenth Dynasty calcite vessels that combined the features of a human woman with those of the goddess Taweret. The goddess' flat breasts, swollen belly, and stubby legs characterize these anthropomorphic vessels.[1]

Beyond its basic form, each vessel is unique. Some, for example, wear a Hathoric coiffure, while others, as this example) wear their hair in plaits down their backs, forming the handle of the vessel. Moreover, the figure rests her hands either on the swell of her stomach or slightly below, on her abdomen. In addition, on many examples, the subject wears a subtle smile and conveys a sense of quiet tranquility.

These vessels likely once contained salve used by pregnant women to ease the strain of pregnancy, reduce stretch marks, and prevent miscarriage. Specifically, Egyptologist Emma Brunner-Traut has suggested that the mixture was composed of a yet-unidentified substance and *behen* oil from moringa trees which was often used by Egyptians because of its stability and perfume-fixation properties.[2] Moreover, calcite may have been chosen for these vessels because the natural bands of color resemble stretch marks. Finally, Taweret's form might have imbued the ointment with her magical protective powers.

It has been suggested that this corpus was related to a group of contemporary vessels that took the form of a mother nursing her child.[3] Their production was rather limited (ca. 1450–1350 B.C.), and they probably derived from a single workshop. In contrast to the pregnancy vessels, the nursing vessels were believed to have once held breast milk.   EVM

NOTE

[1] Morris, "Vase," p. 237.

[2] Brunner-Traut, "Gravidenflasche"; Le Poole, "Behen Oil."

[3] For examples, see Doll, "Bottle in the Form of a Pregnant Woman," p. 293.

PUBLISHED

Brunner-Traut, "Gravidenflasche," p. 37, pl. 7a; Romano, "Jar in the Form of a Woman," p. 63.

56, side view

57. PECTORAL

Light blue-glazed faience
Ptolemaic period, 332–30 B.C.
By Exchange with the Metropolitan Museum of Art, 1950
H: 8.7; W: 8.1 cm
OIM 18286

Pectorals were worn over the breast (see cat. no. 19) or sown into mummy wrappings for protection. This example was used for protection during childbirth. The incised decoration depicts the goddesses Taweret and Hatmehyet and a (possibly pregnant) woman. Hatmehyet, a fish goddess worshipped at Mendes in the Nile Delta after the Twenty-first Dynasty (ca. 1069–945 B.C.), was, in the local mythology, the mother of the local manifestation of Horus. She is depicted on this pectoral wearing her fish emblem on her head. Together with Taweret, a goddess associated with childbirth, she offers protection to the pregnant woman as she worships them. The lower right corner of the pectoral has been restored.   EVM

58–60. GROUP OF FERTILITY AMULETS

58. BES AMULET

Blue-glazed faience
Late Period, Dynasties 25–31, 747–332 B.C.
Gift of Mrs. Helen Swift Neilson, 1944
H: 4.1; W: 1.7; D: 0.6 cm
OIM 17500

59. TAWERET AMULET

Blue-glazed faience
Late Period, Dynasties 25–31, 747–332 B.C.
Purchased in Paris, 1919
H: 5.0 cm
OIM 10089

59 58

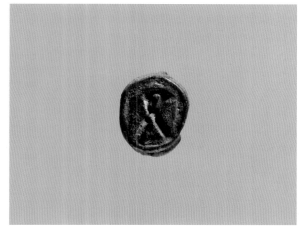

60, view of bottom

60. FROG AMULET

Purple-glazed faience with brown eyes
New Kingdom, Dynasty 18, reigns of Ay and Horemheb,
ca. 1325–1295 B.C.
Medinet Habu, Temple of Ay
Excavated by the Oriental Institute
H: 1.0; W: 0.9; D: 0.9 cm
OIM 14948

Childbirth was an extremely dangerous time for both women and newborn children. As a result, a complex system of beliefs was founded on notions of fertility and protection. Within this system, certain deities were commonly associated with childbirth, including Bes, Heqet, and Taweret, whose powers were invoked by means of magical objects. For example, amulets representing the goddesses Taweret and Heqet and the god Bes were worn as protection from malevolent forces that might seek to harm pregnant women and newborn children.

Bes and Taweret figure prominently in domestic and household religion, and images of them have been found in private homes. They are often grouped together because their representations are considered grotesque and terrifying. Bes, for example, is depicted as a dwarf with a leonine head and tail and a plumed headdress. Taweret is depicted as a hippopotamus with leonine arms and legs and a crocodile tail; she sometimes wears the double-plumed Hathoric headdress. Although terrifying, women and children wore their amulets in life for magical protection.

Frogs symbolized regeneration in ancient Egypt. Thus, Heqet, in her zoomorphic form, was worshipped as a goddess associated with childbirth. Moreover, in the Egyptian story of the creation of mankind, Heqet the frog is depicted crouched beside the potter's wheel as Khnum shaped the first humans. Finally, in the Middle Kingdom, she acted as a midwife in the Tale of the Royal Children of the Papyrus Westcar: "Isis placed herself in front of the woman, Nephthys behind her, and Heqet hastened the birth."

The goddess is depicted here in scaraboid form as a crouching frog with an upraised head and bulging eyes, a trend that began by the late Old Kingdom.[1] The underside of such amulets typically included an inscription or scene. The Oriental Institute frog has the *s3* hieroglyphic sign (meaning "protection") carved on its base. Other examples have the *djed* pillar (meaning "stability") or the ankh sign (meaning "life") EVM

NOTE

[1] Andrews, *Amulets of Ancient Egypt*, p. 63.

PUBLISHED

Teeter, *Scarabs, Scaraboids, Seals, and Seal Impressions*, p. 118, no. 194, pl. 52e.

61. ORACULAR AMULETIC DECREE

Papyrus, ink
Third Intermediate Period, Dynasties 22–23,
ca. 945–715 B.C.
Thebes, Purchased in Luxor, 1932
L: 92.0; W: 6.5 cm
OIM 25622a–d

In the Twenty-second and Twenty-third Dynasties, divine oracles promising specific individuals long life, prosperity, good health, and protection from malevolent forces were recorded on papyrus. These papyri were then rolled up and enclosed in wooden or metal cylinders which were worn as amulets suspended around the neck. As official divine decrees they were official temple products, not the product of personal magic.

The Oriental Institute papyrus, originally one long strip but now in four pieces, records the words of the goddess Nekhbet on behalf of the Lady Taibakhori of Thebes. The text is written in hieratic and is read from right to left:[1]

> Nekhbet, the very great goddess from the beginning of creation, said: "I shall keep safe Taibakhori, this daughter of Tetisheri, she who is also called Sherinihi, my servant and my ward. I shall keep her healthy in her flesh and her bones. I shall protect her and I shall look after her. I shall be between her and any sickness. I shall grant her life, health, and a great and goodly old age. I shall cause her eyes to see; I shall cause her ears to hear; I shall cause her strength to flourish. I shall open her mouth to eat and I shall open her mouth to drink. I shall cause her to eat in order to live and I shall cause her to drink in order to be healthy. I shall cause her to be completely satisfied with a happy life on earth. I shall keep healthy her whole body — every limb — and her entire frame from her head to her soles. I shall keep her safe from every evil intention of every god and every goddess resident in heaven, earth, or the underworld. I shall save her from divine wrath.... I shall save her from every action of a demon and every interference of a demon. I shall save her from every demon of every sort who is in heaven, earth, or the underworld. I shall not let them approach her vicinity at all. I shall save her from every Evil Eye. I shall save her from all Syrian magic. I shall save her from all foreign magic of every sort in the entire earth.... I shall save her from the bite of a snake; I shall save her from the bite of scorpions.... I shall save her from every accident and every abomination at every stage of her journey that

she will make by ship, horse, or on foot.... I shall keep healthy the ten fingers of her hands.... I shall keep healthy her ten toes.... I shall keep healthy her entire frame from her head to her soles.

Nekhbet, the very great goddess from the beginning of creation, said: "As for every matter which has been set down in this written oracle, together with what might have been forgotten to be set down in it, I shall render them beneficial to Taibakhori, the daughter of Tetisheri, she who is also called Sherinihi, every single day." EVM

NOTE

[1] For the full text, see Edwards, *Oracular Amuletic Decrees*, p. 107. The translation given here is adapted from text prepared by Robert Ritner for the Oriental Institute Joseph and Mary Grimshaw Egyptian Gallery in 1999.

PUBLISHED

Edwards, *Oracular Amuletic Decrees*, pp. 107–10.

THE SOCIAL, ECONOMIC, AND LEGAL STATUS OF WOMEN IN ANCIENT EGYPT

Janet H. Johnson

The societal roles of men and women in ancient Egypt were very different, but both participated in the economic life of their society and they had, basically, the same legal status. This combination of roles produced a culture that was unique in the ancient Near East and remained unique through much of pre-modern Western civilization. Most of the information we have about life in ancient Egypt comes from literary texts (stories, wisdom literature, religious texts) and non-literary texts (especially, for our purposes, letters and legal documents), or representations produced by and for elite males, so we know a fair amount about wealthy families but relatively little about the vast majority of Egyptian families who farmed the land and paid their taxes without leaving extensive traces. Thus, much of this discussion is based on materials that relate specifically to elite women (such as Meresamun) and men, not all Egyptians. Archaeological work on settlement sites should provide welcome information about non-elites. The potential distinction between the ideal (the literary) and the "real" (the documentary) makes it important for us to combine both sets of data in our analysis.

Gender roles were quite distinct, at least among these elites about whom we know the most. Both men and women were expected to marry and have a family (see fig. 48). The Instructions of Any — a New Kingdom text intended to teach young men how to behave in life and the world of government service — says: "It is proper to make people. Happy the man whose people are many, he is saluted on account of his progeny."[1] The children would support them in their old age (there was no social security) and carry out the necessary funerary rituals after they died. If a couple couldn't have children, they could adopt: "As for him who has no children, he adopts an orphan instead [to] bring him up. It is his [the adopted child's] responsibility to pour water onto your hands [i.e., carry out traditional funerary rites] as one's own eldest son."[2] The gods were also thought to form families, usually triads: male/father, female/mother, and child, the most famous of which is perhaps Amun–Mut–Khonsu worshipped in the Karnak temple in Thebes, modern Luxor.

But while elite men had jobs in the world of government and the temples (fig. 49), women stayed home, ran the household (fig. 50), and raised the children. Although portions of modern society denigrate this role, it involves, and involved, significant responsibility, perhaps especially in a wealthy household with numerous servants and quantities of goods coming in and going out. The only public job an elite woman might normally have was as a musician associated with a temple. By contrast, non-elite women are found holding a number of jobs (see cat. nos. 71–72). Although we do not know much about Meresamun herself, the status and possible responsibilities of women with her title, Singer in the Interior of the Temple of Amun, are indicated by other examples of women with this title who are clearly members of important Theban families and/or work with or for people of very great importance. One woman with that title, Diesehebsed, is portrayed on a fragment from her tomb (fig. 15). She is shown behind and, apparently, assisting Amenirdis I, the God's Wife of Amun who was the daughter of the Twenty-fifth Dynasty king Taharqa and had been appointed by the king to run the Theban area on behalf of the ruling Kushite (Nubian) dynasty. Diesehebsed's brother, Montuemhat, who held the titles Mayor of

FIGURE 48. Family of the dwarf Seneb, including Seneb, his wife, and their two children. That Seneb is a dwarf has not materially affected the family's self-presentation. Giza, Dynasties 5–6, ca. 2345 B.C. Egyptian Museum, Cairo JdE 51280. Photo: George B. Johnson

FIGURE 49. Neferrenpet at work in the Treasury of Pharaoh. Neferrenpet, the treasurer, is shown seated on a nice chair with his feet on a footstool, wearing an elaborate outfit and carrying a scribal palette as a "badge of office." He is shown much larger than the men dressed in kilts who are working in the office for him, weighing goods, while they, in turn, are much larger than the naked men shown carrying goods to the storerooms under the direction of the medium-sized kilted man supervising them. Tomb of Neferrenpet (Theban Tomb 178), Dynasty 19, ca. 1295–1069 B.C. Photo: C. F. Nims

Thebes and Fourth Priest of Amun, was the effective ruler of Thebes.

This distinction in gender roles is also reflected in Egyptian art. Women are shown as having light (yellow) skin, presumably because they stayed inside and out of the sun, while men are shown as having dark red skin, presumably because they were outside and subject to tanning (fig. 48). Similarly, the relative importance of individuals shown in a scene is indicated by their size, with the more important people frequently being shown larger, sometimes much larger, than other individuals and relatively unimportant individuals being shown very small (fig. 49).

In scenes showing husband and wife, the husband is frequently much larger than the wife. In the example shown in figure 50, the man's head is higher than his wife's even though he is sitting and she is standing. This reflects partly the actual physical size of the individuals but also their relative importance; this monument is the husband's, he is the center of attention, and he is shown the largest. But because it seems to have been considered unseemly for a woman to be shown larger than a man, monuments dedicated by and on behalf of a woman in her own right and not as someone's wife usually do not show her husband, even if she had one. Good wives are portrayed in literature and in letters as taking care of their husbands. Thus, in the New Kingdom Story of the Two Brothers, the wife of the elder brother is expected to have the house lit and be prepared to pour water on her husband's hands on his return from work. Similarly, in figure 50, the

husband sits on his chair while his wife serves him. But with this duty to serve the husband came the responsibility for running the house, including directing the servants. This responsibility is reflected in the Story of the Two Brothers by the fact that it is the wife who has the keys to the storeroom where the seed grain is stored.

One element of self-identity[3] came with occupation, which provided or reflected one's status. It can be noted that many titles in ancient Egypt served not so

FIGURE 50. The household of Djehutynefer. Djehutynefer and his wife appear to the left. Their home is filled with servants. Tomb of Djehutynefer (Theban Tomb 104), New Kingdom, Dynasty 18, reign of Amenhotep II, ca. 1427 B.C. After Badawy, *History of Egyptian Architecture*, p. 16

much as job descriptions (e.g., "scribe," "laundryman") but as status markers, showing where one fit in society, for example, "servant of god X," indicating that the individual worked for the temple of the god X and that this institution could be called on to support him in time/case of trouble; or *nbt pr* "mistress of the house" (discussed below). Since both government and temples were organized hierarchically, age, length of service, and rank to which a man had risen were all part of his status and self-identity. Such status and self-identity spread from the man to his wife; the Instructions of Any note, "A woman is asked about her husband, a man is asked about his rank/profession/office."[4] Since professions and jobs were frequently handed down through families (see cat. no. 2 and fig. 6), one's kin were also part of one's identity. There is little evidence in the preserved record of either men or women challenging these gendered expectations; both men and women seem to have been socialized to put the needs of the community above the development of the individual/individuality.

LEGAL STATUS

Although the social roles of men and women were sharply different, their legal status was amazingly similar. Both women and men could claim the status of (*rmt*) *nmh* "free man/woman/citizen,"[5] indicating that the person was not bound to an institution or another individual but was free to act in his or her own name. Similarly, both women and men were held accountable for their own actions in terms of both civil and criminal law. We have, for example, records of criminal charges of theft brought against various women[6]; both women and men could be interrogated and accused of hiding information about thefts. A New Kingdom ostracon includes the statement, "The anger of God happened to me, so I (a female) confessed I saw the woman [personal name] steal it." Women as well as men found guilty of treason were executed.[7]

Both women and men could be party to a legal document; both could bring a court case or be sued; and both could serve as witnesses in a court case or to a legal document.[8] That women very rarely did actually serve as witnesses reflects the fact that witnesses normally were selected from among individuals present in the area where the case was being heard or the document drawn up and this, being public space, was territory filled with men, not women. In some examples of

women serving as witnesses, the women were relatives of parties to the document who have a vested interest in the case, and probably intentionally came to the site where the legal transaction would take place specifically to serve as witness. As in any legal system, clout (in this case men's normal participation in the public world, including networking with other men) could give an advantage to one group over another, so that, for instance, women may have been less likely to instigate a legal case against a man than vice versa. But in Egyptian society, clout could also derive from wealth and status, and an elite woman may have held an edge over a non-elite man in any legal situation.

In addition, both women and men could own (and acquire and dispose of) property, both real and personal, in their own name; women did not need to act through a male relative, as they did in many other ancient societies. An interesting archive of private contracts from the reign of Darius I, early in the Persian empire (ca. 500 B.C.), somewhat later than when Meresamun lived, documents the buying, selling, and leasing of land by a woman named Tsenhor.[9] Tsenhor was a member of a family of *choachytes*, people who carried out burial ceremonies for the deceased and were paid to look after their tombs and mummies. This collection of documents shows women, especially Tsenhor and her daughter, buying and selling land, slaves, and animals and dealing with inheritance (on which see further discussion below). For women owning real estate and being recognized as legitimate owners (and tax payers) on such property, one can cite Papyrus Wilbour, a long New Kingdom text recording "taxes" due on farmland; each piece of land is identified by owner and (if different) by the person working the land. Of the 2,110 parcels of land for which the name of the owner is preserved, women are listed as owners of 228, just over 10 percent; the land frequently is described as being worked by their children. However these women originally acquired this land (whether by inheritance as widows or as daughters of men who had acquired the land as payment for military service, as has been suggested, or by some other means), what is significant is that they hold title to the land and bear responsibility for assessments due. Texts more nearly contemporary with Meresamun also show women owning and transferring land. An excellent example is the Apanage Stela,[10] which records sixteen plots of land that the owner of the stela had purchased, two of which he obtained from women.

This quite unusual combination of gender differentiation with legal equality seems to be tied to the Egyptian recognition of duality in all things. Geographically and politically, Egypt was the combination of Upper Egypt and Lower Egypt, the red land (the desert) and the black land (the cultivation). The king was the King of Upper and Lower Egypt, he could be shown wearing a crown of Upper Egypt, a crown of Lower Egypt, or a double crown as King of Upper and Lower Egypt. Important state institutions came in pairs — the double granary of Upper and Lower Egypt which represented the state's involvement with the economy — and, in religion, deities came in pairs. For every male deity there was a female who completed him; it was the pairing which made the divineness complete.[11] Men's and women's roles in society were different, but both were vital to society and not to be denigrated. In the New Kingdom Instructions of Any, Any advises, "Do not control your wife in her house, when you know she is efficient; Don't say to her: 'Where is it? Get it!' when she has put it in the right place. Let your eye observe in silence, then you recognize her skill. It is joy when your hand is with her, there are many who don't

know this. If a man desists from strife at home, he will not encounter its beginning. Every man who founds a household should hold back the hasty heart."[12] A later text, perhaps composed during the period when Meresamun lived, put it succinctly, "A woman knows her own business."[13]

Women not only had an important role to play in society, they had an important role to play in the training of the next generation of society. The Instructions of Any advised men to honor their mothers because, among other things, "When she sent you to school, and you were taught to write, she kept watching over you daily, with bread and beer in her house."[14]

The men who wrote the documents and had the tombs decorated stressed their own roles and included women when the role of women intersected with their own world. This is seen especially in the inclusion of wives in the tombs not only because of their role in the family but because of their role in the tomb owner's future regeneration in the afterlife. The sexuality of the female, and her fertility, were used to ensure that a deceased male would be revived in the afterlife and live "happily ever after." Although there are presentations of the deceased male with erect phallus, indicating that he is both alive and sexually active after death, tomb reliefs far more frequently represent a sexually alluring female to indicate that the tomb owner has/will come through the judgment day and come to life again "on the far side." It has been noted frequently that standard presentations of women highlight their sexuality/fertility. Their breasts are shown as exposed or highlighted, their pubic areas are stressed even through clothing, and they wear elaborate hairdos or wigs[15] and much jewelry (fig. 51).

PROPERTY AND MARRIAGE

As noted, both women and men could own property; in addition, both women and men brought property into their marriage. This included both personal property such as clothing, toilet articles, and jewelry as well as home furnishings (cat. nos. 21–47).[16] But both women and men could also bring real property to the marriage. A classic example which dates from just slightly after the time of Meresamun involves the daughter of a man named Padi-Isis.[17] Padi-Isis had moved his family out of Thebes during a time of civil unrest. He became an important civil servant and priest of the local god in a small town near the Faiyum. When order had been

FIGURE 51. Sketch of a royal woman wearing an elaborate headdress, transparent dress, and broad collar, and carrying scepters. This may be a preliminary sketch for a scene in the tomb of Queen Isis, the mother of Ramesses VI. Even on a monument made in honor of a prominent woman, she may be shown in attire that accentuates her body and with symbols stressing her femininity and fertility. Dynasty 20, reign of Ramesses VI, ca. 1143–1136 B.C. OIM 17006

restored in the country and power was returning to Theban officials and priests, he decided to take his family back to Thebes in order to get his sons into the power structure there. But he did not want to give up his standing and wealth in the small town where they had been living. Therefore, he arranged for a young priest from Thebes, whose family had ties to the same cult in Thebes that Padi-Isis's family had ties with, to court his daughter. When the couple married, Padi-Isis gave his daughter one share of the income from the local temple (with this share came the rights and responsibilities of serving as priest in the local temple, a job exercised by the daughter's new husband) and also gave his daughter the family house in the small town. If this practice of giving a daughter at marriage what may have been her inheritance, including real estate, was at all common, then the title that is used to indicate married women, *nbt pr* "mistress of the house," may not only indicate the woman's role in charge of the house but also justify a second translation of the title "owner of a house" (cat. no. 64).[18]

Men had three potential sources of wealth/property. As expressed by Nakht-Mut, the owner of Cairo Statue 42208 (fig. 52) discussed below, "I am the possessor of property from my father and my mother and what I [acquired with my own] hands. The rest is as a favor of the king for my service in my time." Since most (elite) women did not have a job outside the home for which they would be rewarded/paid by the king, they had only two sources of wealth or property: inheritance and what they could earn by, for instance, weaving and selling textiles (see cat. nos. 65–71). Because the husband was expected to participate in the public world, he assumed responsibility for supporting the family and handling the family's possessions/wealth. He had the legal right to sell, on behalf of the family, an item brought to the family by the wife at marriage, but if he did so, he had the responsibility to replace it with something of equal value.[19] There was a concept of communal or family property acquired by the couple during the marriage, distinct from the personal property of either the wife or the husband.

The economic disadvantage to women resulting from their exclusion from the regular/official work force and their resulting economic dependency on men (husband, father, brother, son) seems to have been one of the factors leading to the development of what are called "annuity documents" (literally, "documents of causing/allowing one to live"; cat. no. 62), by which a man guaranteed to support his wife for as long as she wanted him to do so. The oldest example of an annuity document to which we have reference was written about 760 B.C. That the social, economic, and legal situation underlying these documents was present in Egyptian society long before that time is suggested by a Middle Kingdom document (nearly 1,500 years earlier) which has been interpreted as serving many of the same functions as the Late Period annuity documents.[20]

The annuity documents, written by the husband to the wife, acknowledged receipt by the man from the woman of a certain amount of money and in turn guaranteed that he would provide her with a set amount of grain and a set sum of money for clothing and other necessities every year, whether she was still living with him or not. He did not have the right to return the money to her and stop the payments, but if she so desired, she could ask for the money back and he was obligated to return it, thereby ending his commitment to provide food and clothing. Written into the contract was the stipulation that, if he reneged on his payments for food and clothing, she had the ongoing legal right to collect the money for them from him.

A second major impetus behind the creation of these documents was their further proclamation that all the children that the wife had born or would bear to the husband were his heirs and all his property, both what he had at the time of writing the contract and any that he acquired afterward, were entailed as security for her annual support and to be inherited by their children. All their children had the right to inherit from both of them (personal property and family/communal property) unless one parent specifically disinherited one or more children.[21]

If a couple divorced (divorce could be instigated by either the husband or the wife), each partner kept his or her own personal property, including real property, and the family or joint property was divided between the husband and wife, usually at a ratio of two-thirds to the husband, one-third to the wife. Both were then free to remarry. However, the legal provisions of the annuity contract that entailed the husband's property as the inheritance of her/their children remained in effect. Thus, if a man did remarry, he would have to get his ex-wife or "eldest son" (see further below) to agree to let him use any property already entailed for the children from the first marriage as security for the position of the second wife and future inheritance of any children of the second marriage.

This is seen clearly in several Ptolemaic-period annuity documents, including those cited in the so-called Family Archive from Siut. In those texts, a man who had married a second time and written annuity documents for each of his wives got his eldest son, by his first wife, to sign his annuity document for his second wife, thereby agreeing to the father/husband using a portion of his wealth to endow his second wife (after having entailed a larger portion of his wealth for the children of the first wife). The wife of the eldest son sued the son of the second wife to try to reclaim all of her father-in-law's property based on her own annuity document written to her by the eldest son, her husband. That it was the wife who took action probably reflects the fact that the husband had tried earlier and had his case thrown out of court. But in this case, the courts decided that, because the eldest son had approved the distribution among the siblings and his father's second wife, the documents were legal, and the younger son (and daughter) were the legal owners of the property inherited from their father through this annuity document.

INHERITANCE

One area that exemplifies the social, economic, and legal situation of women revolves around inheritance. In many cases, a(n elderly) parent would write (a) contract(s) to his/her child(ren), passing on his/her real property, akin to a modern will.[22] But if a person died without having done so, there were specific rules for inheritance, spelled out in the so-called Hermopolis Legal Code, a collection of case law, the preserved copy of which was written in the Ptolemaic era, but whose occasional archaic writings suggest that it was probably compiled during the Late Period. This Legal Code reflects residual rights of primogeniture since it says the eldest son acts on behalf of his siblings. It is his responsibility to undertake proper burial of his parents and carry out all the proper funerary rituals. For this expense, in time and money, he was awarded one extra share in the parents' wealth. But the Hermopolis Legal Code also states specifically that it can be a daughter who acts as "eldest son," who undertakes the responsibilities, and who receives the extra share as inheritance. In addition, this Legal Code also envisions the possibility that a parent can pick any child (female or male, eldest, youngest, or in the middle) to serve as "eldest son."[23]

But some individuals chose a more public way to make their inheritance plans known. Texts on a statue[24] of a man named Nakht-Mut of the Twenty-second Dynasty (the dynasty during which it is suggested that Meresamun lived), record not only his praise of the god Amun, the main god worshipped in the Karnak temple, but also his intention to have his daughter Tasherien-Mut (nicknamed Shepen-Isis) be his sole heir and recipient of all property he currently owned and everything he might acquire. The statue shows Nakht-Mut, dressed as a priest with a simulated animal skin over his shoulder, holding up a stela (fig. 52). His wife is shown in relief on the right side of the stela, supporting his decision. Their daughter is shown on the left, acknowledging their generosity. The text reads, in part:

> Praising Amun-Re, king of the gods, lord of heaven, lord of the land, lord of the water, lord of the mountains, lord of the oceans, ... by the Fourth Priest of Amun[25] (whose name is) Nakht-Mut, who says:

> "I say this to you as praise and prayer that you come to me quickly. I call on behalf of my daughter ... who is in my heart, she being excellent for me, ..., (whose name is) Tasherien-Mut, who is called Shepen-Isis,

FIGURE 52. Statue of Nakht-Mut incised with a text by which he and his wife leave their estate to their daughter. Dynasty 22, ca. 945–715 B.C. Cairo 42208. From Legrain, *Catalogue Général*, pl. 15

born to (the woman) Nes-Mut, ... in order that you make permanent for her the transfer document[26] of everything which I gave to her ... in city and in country, consisting of servants, cattle, household goods, and all valuable objects.... No other son or daughter shall say 'Give me the like!' You shall not allow her to lose any extra (property) which (comes) into my house after today[27] ... like the Great God said: 'Let every man make the determination of his (own) property!' I am the possessor of property from my father and my mother and what I [acquired with my own] hands. The rest is as a favor of the King for my service in my time.... You are the good protector of the trusted one, who answers the call of the sleeping (i.e., the deceased). Thus you should fight against the one who will fight against him in the future.[28] Send your arrow ... against them in order to wipe out their breath.... It will be against all great people, all brothers, all people who will trespass against her in the future,[29] concerning everything which I gave her and everything which I gave her children...."[30]

The Mistress of the House[31] (whose name is) Tines-Mut,[32] who says:

"(O god) Amun, you are the molder of gods and men. You are the strength of those who live and the protection of those who are dead.... Come to me, I am your servant! Act excellently for our daughter Shepen-Isis! Let her seize this property and kill anyone who will trespass against her![33] You are the protector of the future."

The daughter Tasherien-Mut, who is called Shepen-Isis, who says:

"What is the God of a person except his father and his mother? ... The one who handed over to me is one who loved me, my (god) Khnum and my (goddess) Meskhenet.[34] I seized everything they made for me for they are justified before god. May the gods act according as you (plural)[35] testified forever!"

Thus, women and men both inherited both real and movable property from both their parents and, in turn, passed along both real and movable property to their children, both daughters and sons (biological or adoptive). Note that in most cases, real property was not actually divided among the children, but, rather, each of the children received a share of undivided real property (see cat. no. 63). It is assumed that this was done to maintain the real property intact and to avoid the division and subdivision of land which would lead to ownership of plots of land too small

to work productively. Likewise, houses could not be literally subdivided beyond, perhaps, halves or thirds/ quarters, but shares could, and frequently did, result in siblings owning one-sixteenth or one-eighteenth shares of a structure. Frequently, one sibling would take responsibility for managing such property, making sure that the structure and/or land was properly maintained and every owner of a share received his or her fair share of income and, presumably, paid his or her fair share of maintenance costs. A famous example of management of joint property by a sibling, the New Kingdom inscription of Mes,[36] has a woman acting as the "agent" for her siblings; it has been suggested that perhaps this woman was chosen to handle this family property because she was especially adept at such things but also partly because, as a woman, she did not have a full-time job outside the home and therefore had more time than her brothers to dedicate to handling the property. The Persian-period archive of the woman Tsenhor[37] includes examples of siblings confirming their inheritance of property from both their parents; from the later Ptolemaic period, we have a number of examples of re-sorting among siblings in order to coalesce small shares of real property into larger, more useful, holdings.[38]

An interesting, if difficult, text from the period when Meresamun lived relates that a man inherited valuable property, in this case a well and the water flowing from it in the Dakhla Oasis, where water was at a premium.[39] The text is preserved on a stela discovered in that oasis in 1894 (fig. 53). The stela records the official visit to Dakhla Oasis by officials sent by King Sheshonq to restore order and central government control of the oasis after a period of "war and turmoil(?)." A group of officials surveyed all the water sources in the oasis to determine which belonged to the state/pharaoh and which belonged to private individuals. They determined that one particular well, the water coming from it, and the land watered by it had belonged to a woman named Tayuḥenut and now it belonged to her sole legitimate heir, Nysu-Bastet, the owner of the stela.[40] The legal ownership was verified by checking the records made in year 19 of King Psusennes, in the Twenty-first Dynasty, and it was confirmed by an oracle from the god Seth (see cat. nos. 15–16). The stela ends with the confirmation that this well and these water rights are his to pass along to his heirs, specifically his wife and children, and they, in turn, to their heirs. The text relates, in part:

Year 5, 4th month of Winter, day 16, of King Sheshonq, beloved of (the god) Amun. On this day came(?) the son of the Prince of the Ma,[41] the chief official of lands, the priest of (the goddess) Ḥathor of (the city of) Diospolis, the priest of (the god) Ḥorus and (the goddess) Sekhmet(?) of (the city of) Pedjodj, the priest of (the god) Seth of the Oasis, the overseer of inundated lands, the overseer of plantations(?), the prince of the two lands of the Oasis, (whose name is) Wayhes,[42] he being in the town of Sawahet, after Pharaoh had sent him to restore order in the Oasis-land, after he had found it in a state of war and turmoil(?). On the day when he went to inspect the flowing wells and the (other) wells which are in Sawahet, ... he arrived to see the well of flowing water of (i.e., named) Weben[-Ra], after the priest of (the god) Seth (whose name is) Nysu-Bastet, the son of Padi, had spoken before him saying:

"Behold, a sheet of flood-water has been let loose and is here in the neighborhood of this flowing well of (i.e., named) Weben-Ra. Examine it, namely this [well of] (the district called) Per-Ra in whose neighborhood you are, for (it is) a private[43] well, and it belongs to my mother (whose name is) Tayuḥenut, whose mother was Ḥenutnetjeru."[44]

Then the priest and prince Wayhes said to him: "Stand in the presence of (the god) Seth [and claim] it."[45]

In year 5, 4th month of Winter, day 25, on the day when the noble god Seth, great of strength, the son of (the goddess) Nut, this great god, was caused to appear at his feast "Beauty of Daytime," the prince Wayhes stood in the Presence. Then Seth, the great god, said: "Nysu-Bastet, the son of Padi, is in the right. This flood-water which is to the northwest of the well of flowing water of (i.e., named) Weben-Ra, this well of (the district called) Per-Ra, which is in (the town of) Sawahet, is the property of his mother Tayuḥenut. Confirm it for him today."

The conclusion of the central government official who was making the inspection was that "These are private waters, and there is no water of Pharaoh[46] among them."

The well, the well water, and the land watered by the well, were confirmed to him and to his heirs because there was "no other son of private status[47] belonging to Tayuḥenut who shall have a share in them except Nysu-Bastet, the son of Padi.'"

Thus spoke Seth, the great god, before very many witnesses. List thereof: ...

In summary, men and women had very different social roles to play in ancient Egypt, at least among the elite; men had jobs or professions outside the house, in the public sphere, while women stayed home and

FIGURE 53. Stela from Dakhla Oasis inscribed with a text that relates that a valuable well belonged to a man who had in turn inherited it from his mother. The scene at the top depicts the government official Wayhes, holding what has been described as a lamp, and the Priest of Seth Nysu-Bastet, the owner of the well and the water, in front of what may be the place where the oracle of Seth was given. The women depicted probably include Nysu-Bastet's mother, and perhaps grandmother, through whom he inherited the well and water, and perhaps his wife and daughter, as his potential heirs. Women playing rectangular frame drums appear at the bottom right. Dynasty 22, reign of Sheshonq I(?), ca. 940 B.C.

ran the house and raised the children, in the private sphere. Some women, including or especially those from the highest ranks of the elite, had an important role to play in religion, providing music necessary for temple and, apparently, funerary ritual. Meresamun's title clearly identifies her as a member of the Theban elite, probably related to men who held important jobs in the temple and governmental hierarchy. Her coffin indicates wealth in the family, also indicated by her title. She would have been in charge of her own house, (at least partially) responsible for the education and training of her children to carry on her and her husband's traditions, and a woman with "clout" in Thebes in the Twenty-second Dynasty. It is exciting to try to reconstruct what her physical world was like while considering what her mental or emotional assumptions may have been. We hope we have raised some questions which will make Meresamun and her life more alive, and more interesting, to contemporary people — people who can recognize in her some of the same hopes, dreams, and, perhaps, frustrations that we encounter on a regular basis.

NOTES

[1] Translation from Lichtheim, *Literature*, vol. 2, p. 136.

[2] Ostracon Berlin 10627, translation from Wente, *Letters*, pp. 149, 230 (no. 206).

[3] For women's sexual identity as an important aspect of their personal identity, see Roth, "Father Earth," pp. 194–95.

[4] Translation from Lichtheim, *Literature*, vol. 2, p. 140.

[5] The term translated "free" means something such as "unencumbered"; it is used in the so-called Adoption Papyrus (New Kingdom, published in Gardiner, "Adoption Extraordinary") to indicate that individuals who had been born slaves had been released from bondage by their owner and were now free subjects of Pharaoh. In the Persian-period archive of a woman named Tsenhor (see further below), "to act as a *nmḥ*" (*ir nmḥ*) is contrasted with "to act as a slave" (*ir bꜣk*) (for discussion, see Pestman, *Tsenhor*, pp. 65–66, n. 6). In the Dakhla Stela quoted later in this essay, *šr nmḥ* is the term used to identify a son/child who is legally independent and thus eligible to inherit, and "*nmḥ* waters" are contrasted with "waters of Pharaoh," that is, "private" versus "crown" property (see Gardiner, "Dakhleh Stela," p. 21). For further discussion, see Mattha and Hughes, *Demotic Legal Code*, p. 70, note to line 1; and Ritner, "Legal Terminology," p. 350.

[6] In one case, a woman who had stolen property was found guilty not only of the theft, which would normally have had to be repaid at a value of two or three to one, but also of swearing a false oath (in the name of the king); as a result, she was held in custody to have her punishment decided by the appropriate official of the central administration.

[7] For general discussion of the evidence from the New Kingdom workmen's village of Deir el-Medina, see McDowell, *Jurisdiction*.

[8] For example, the so-called Adoption Papyrus (see note 5, above) records, in part one, a man's adoption of his wife as his daughter (he having no other children), so that she could inherit all his property. The man notes specifically that he is disinheriting his siblings (who would otherwise have inherited from him if he had no children) and that he made this bequest to his wife "before his sister," presumably as representative of those siblings; his document was witnessed by several individuals, including one woman whose husband also served as a witness. In the second part of this document, the wife, who has now inherited her husband's property, stipulates that it is her younger brother, who has married the oldest of the slave children born in the family and taken in two younger slave siblings of his wife, together with these slave children (they having "dealt well with me") who will be her heirs, all of them now to be treated as "free men of Pharaoh." The witnesses to this second declaration also include women as well as men. For discussion of a unique New Kingdom ostracon which seems to indicate women serving as members of a court, see McDowell, *Jurisdiction*, p. 160.

[9] See note 5, above.

[10] Stela of Iuwelot, Dynasty 22, Cairo, Egyptian Museum, JdE 31882; a new transliteration, translation, and commentary by Robert Ritner will appear in his forthcoming *The Libyan Anarchy: Documents from Egypt's Third Intermediate Period*. As he noted (personal communication), women are also presented as property holders in other Third Intermediate Period texts, such as the settlement of Henuttawy and the oracular decree for Maatkare.

[11] For a similar interpretation, expressed more theologically, see Roth, "Gender Roles," pp. 212, 217–18; and Roth, "Father Earth, Mother Sky," p. 194.

[12] Translation from Lichtheim, *Literature*, vol. 2, p. 143.

[13] Instructions of 'Onchsheshonqy, translation from Lichtheim, *Literature*, vol. 3, p. 170.

[14] Translation from Lichtheim, *Literature*, vol. 2, p. 141.

[15] The sexual implications of which are incorporated in Egyptian tales, as well.

[16] For discussion of the wide range of women's possessions which are mentioned in annuity documents (on which, see below) as being brought to the marriage by the woman, see Lüddeckens, *Ägyptische Eheverträge*, pp. 288–304.

[17] See Vittmann, *Papyrus Rylands* 9.

[18] Note the large number of women from the Late Period who are recorded on their funerary stelae (see Munro, *Totenstelen*) bearing the title *nbt pr* together with a title as a musician (similar to Meresamun's title as Singer). For a discussion of elite women and their titles in the Late Period, see Johnson, "Women, Wealth and Work."

[19] Demotic distinguishes between the "proprietary right" of a woman's property, which belonged to the woman, and the "right of disposal" of that property, which belonged to her husband. Pestman ("Appearance and Reality" pp. 84–85) discussed what he termed "deceits" when a contract was made in the name of a man for property belonging to his wife. But see the additional comments by Johnson ("Women, Wealth and Work," pp. 1411–16) on whether such practices should actually be understood to involve "deceit."

[20] See Johnson, "Speculations."

[21] The "Will of (the woman) Naunakht" (New Kingdom, published by Černý, "Will of Naunakhte") indicates that an individual could disinherit individual children but could not disinherit all his or her children.

[22] Published by H. Thompson, *Family Archive*.

[23] For examples, see the Persian-period archive of the woman Tsenhor, mentioned in note 5.

[24] Note also the statement by Nakht-Mut on Statue Cairo 42208 (fig. 52), quoted below, "like the great god said, 'Let every man make the determination of his (own) property!'"

[25] Although the title Fourth Priest of Amun does not sound like an especially high-ranking title, it is one of the titles of Montuemhat, who was concurrently mayor of Thebes and effective ruler of the Theban area, as noted above.

[26] Such documents, frequently understood as sales contracts, are known from as early as the Old Kingdom and served to transfer ownership of property from one individual to another, usually someone other than the individual who would inherit if the "seller" died. For discussion, see Logan, "The *Jmyt-pr* Document."

[27] That is, she inherits not only what her father owns at the time the statue was commissioned but also anything which he acquired subsequently, up until his death.

[28] That is, in the afterlife.

[29] People who might try to strip her of her inheritance include "great people" (i.e., influential people), male relatives, and "others."

[30] Note that it is assumed that she will pass along the property to her children. The god is called on to (help) enforce the statue owner's decisions on inheritance. The period during which these individuals lived was a contentious one, which may have led Nakht-Mut to call on the god's help and intervention more than in most similar inscriptions.

[31] *Nbt pr*; for the possible dual implications of this title, see above.

[32] A variant spelling of the mother's name.

[33] Such strong language is unusual and, as noted above, perhaps reflects the unsettled era in which this family lived.

[34] Khnum is the god who fashioned mankind on his potter's wheel and thus a reference to her father. Meskhenet is the goddess of birth and thus a reference to her mother.

[35] Note that she recognizes that both parents were involved in this bequest.

[36] Published by Gardiner, *Inscriptions of Mes*.

[37] See note 5, above.

[38] See, for example, Papyrus Louvre 3266 (Ptolemaic, published by de Cenival, "Acte de renonciation") resorting inherited property between a brother and a sister.

[39] Published by Gardiner, "Dakhla Inscription."

[40] Since Nysu-Bastet is careful to identify the mother of his mother, the implication may be that his mother had, in turn, inherited the well and water rights from her mother.

[41] One of the Libyan tribes which had taken control in the delta and controlled Egypt during the Third Intermediate Period; here it is a reference to central authority.

[42] Note the range of titles that Wayhes uses: priest of various deities, including Seth of the Oasis before whom the oracular judgment takes place; titles indicating his right to survey land (and water) ownership; and, first and foremost, a title tying him to the (new) ruling dynasty in the Nile Valley.

[43] *Nmḥ*; see discussion in note 5, above.

[44] Note identification by (name of) mother (and mother of mother) rather than father when the property belonged to the mother and she, therefore, was the relevant ancestor.

[45] This is a trial by oracle. Although resort to oracular decisions is frequently seen to reflect lack of "hard data" which can condemn or justify an individual or a situation, in this case the oracular decision was based on state records and seems to be a way to reimpose state control on the oasis by means of divine intervention. Care was taken to specify the specific cadastral record (Psusennes, year 19) and the official who made the copy (Ankhaf, the son of Seth-nakht) so that anyone who had any questions or disagreements could go and find the documentation for themselves.

[46] For this distinction between private and state-owned property, see the discussion in note 5.

[47] See discussion in note 5, above.

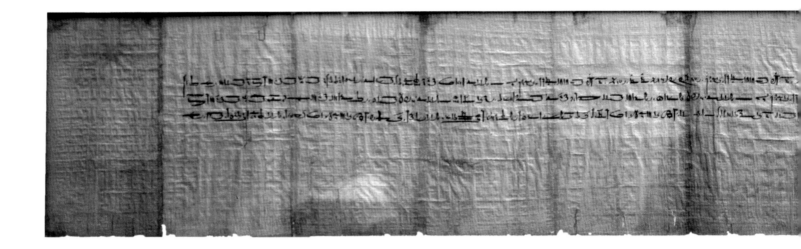

62. ANNUITY CONTRACT

Papyrus, ink
Late Period, Dynasty 30, reign of Nectanebo, between
22 December 365 B.C. and 20 January 364 B.C.
Faiyum, Hawara
Purchased in Cairo, 1932
L: 230; H: 37 cm
OIM 17481

Annuity contracts made by a husband to his wife
appear to have had two major underlying aims: to
assure that the husband will properly support the
wife and her children, and to assure that it is her
children who will be his heirs. In a society in which,
as a norm, men worked and acquired (disposable)
income but women did not, this was an important
guarantor of stability for both the family and the
society.

Although annuity contracts are first attested
in this form during the period of the Persian
empire, they seem to reflect social and financial
relations between husband and wife seen much
earlier. For instance, New Kingdom documents
attest concern with inheritance of property, and it
has even been suggested that a Middle Kingdom
"transfer document" is underpinned by similar
cultural assumptions and norms.[1] Note that these
contracts are not "marriage contracts" in that
they do not provide legitimation for a marriage as
such and do not discuss proper behavior between
husband and wife, or between husband or wife
and other individuals.[2] Almost all such contracts
mention children born by the woman to the man.

Some contracts (including this one) use the future
tense ("children whom you will bear to me"), but
others use both the past tense and the future tense
("children whom you have born to me and whom
you will bear to me"), which may imply that the
contract need not be made at the time of contracting
the marriage but, in some cases, perhaps, after the
woman has proven herself fertile by providing an
heir.

Egyptian legal contracts, although made by one
party to the other, are actually bilateral and subject
to the approval of both parties. If the recipient of the
document did not accept the terms of the contract,
he or she could reject the document and the party
making the document would either have to modify
the terms or give up whatever he/she was trying to
achieve.

This annuity contract was drawn up by a
man named Ankh-merwer on behalf of his wife,
a woman named Peset. All the men mentioned
in the contract[3] bore the title God's Sealer and
Embalmer — a standard title among individuals
who were responsible for mummifying and burying
the deceased. Thus, these men and women are
marrying individuals from the same ranks of society
as themselves and their families, and jobs are kept or
"run" in families. The husband acknowledges receipt
from his wife of thirty pieces of silver of the standard
(for weight and quality) of the Treasury of (the god)
Ptah. He promises to provide her, every year, with
thirty-six sacks of emmer (wheat) and 1.2 pieces of
silver[4] for her subsistence; he further promises to
provide them at whatever house she wishes,[5] without
the legal possibility of defaulting on his debt. It is

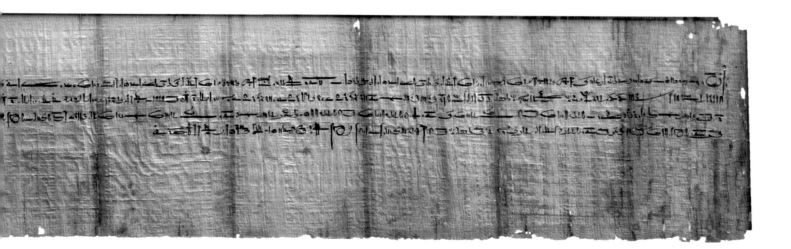

stipulated that the man may not, on his own, return the thirty pieces of silver, that is, the annuity, to the woman and, thereby, cancel his debt. But if the woman asks for her annuity to be returned, the man must do so; in this latter case, the marriage is considered ended and both the woman and the man are free to marry someone else.[6]

Whether or not the couple divorce, one of the major provisions of the contract remained in force: The couple's children are the legal heirs to all the man's property ("that which I possess and that which I shall acquire"), spelled out in this contract to consist of "house, field, courtyard, building plot, male servant, female servant, every animal, every title deed and every free thing[7] in the world which I possess." The contract goes on to specify that everything which he possesses and everything which he will acquire is to serve as the security for this annuity contract. The man making the contract also agrees that he cannot force either his wife or any of the people who served as witnesses to the contract to take an oath concerning the contract[8] anywhere except in the "place in which the judges are."[9] That is, they can be brought to the legitimate place for hearing contests concerning contracts, but they cannot be made to travel long distances to unusual locales to defend her rights. The contract ends with the father of the husband declaring his "satisfaction" with the document and saying, "Accept my son that he may execute this document and fulfill all its obligations!" At the end of the contract is given a list of witnesses who were present and witnessed the agreement between the parties.[10]

It is interesting that this particular document, like several others, ends with a declaration by an interested party, in this case the father of the man who made the contract. As noted above, this is not a formal "marriage contract" and the father is not giving permission for the son to marry. He is formally acknowledging the maker of the contract as his son, and therefore his heir. Since sons did not normally inherit from their fathers until the death of the father, a man whose father was still alive might not have much wealth with which to secure his annuity contract. But if his father subscribes to the contract, claiming him as heir and indicating that he has no problem accepting the marriage and the commitment

62, detail of reverse: list of witnesses

of his son's current and future wealth to this wife and the children she bears his son, then the wife, and the wife's family, can rest assured that, in due time, the husband will inherit from his father and have the wealth to take care of the family in an appropriate manner. The interested party could also be a woman who had a legal claim to property being conveyed, for example, by an ex-husband, who had written her an annuity contract by virtue of which she and her children had gained a vested interest in all her husband's property. It is in the best interests of the ex-husband and the new purchaser of the property for her to renounce her claim at the time the new contract was being made, rather than having her later bring suit against the new owner.[11]

The elegant calligraphic hand used to write this document, the large size of the document with its wide borders on expensive sheets of papyrus, and the care used by the scribe in laying out the text all reflect the amount of time and money this family was willing and able to invest in this formative family document. JHJ

NOTES

[1] Johnson, "Speculations."

[2] Such clauses are found in both the Aramaic and the Greek marriage contracts found from first-millennium B.C. Egypt.

[3] The maker of the contract (the husband), his father, and the father of the wife.

[4] Of the standard (for weight and quality) of those of the Treasury of (the god) Ptah.

[5] This indicates that, even if the woman has left the man and their conjugal home, the man remains liable for providing food and money for clothing (and other essentials).

[6] In some cases a man makes a divorce contract for his wife, specifically stating that he has rejected her as wife and she is free to marry whomever she pleases. In the New Kingdom, a man who divorced his wife had to pay her a monetary penalty (unless he divorced her for cause). This payment would have the same effect as the return of the silver of the annuity stipulated in Late Period annuity contracts. It has even been suggested that the silver which the woman is said to have provided the man in these Late Period annuity contracts is fictional, setting up a situation in which the man accepts a sum as the amount he would have to pay if, in the future, he divorced his wife.

[7] Or, "things of a free man."

[8] That is, swear about specific details of the contract

[9] This legal nicety is spelled out more clearly in the Hermopolis Legal Code, published by Mattha and Hughes, *Demotic Legal Code*.

[10] In this case a list of thirty-six men, most of whom have priestly titles.

[11] See also the discussion of Catalog No. 63.

PUBLISHED

Hughes and Jasnow, *Hawara Papyri*, pp. 9–15, pls. 1–7; Nims, "'Document of Endowment'"; Teeter, *Ancient Egypt*, no. 46.

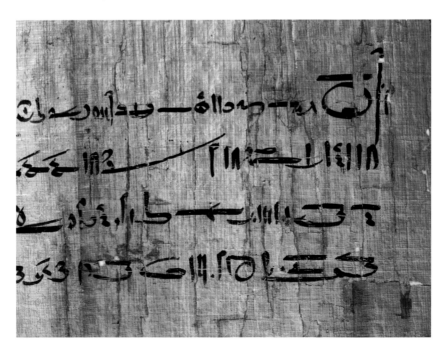

62, detail of calligraphic script

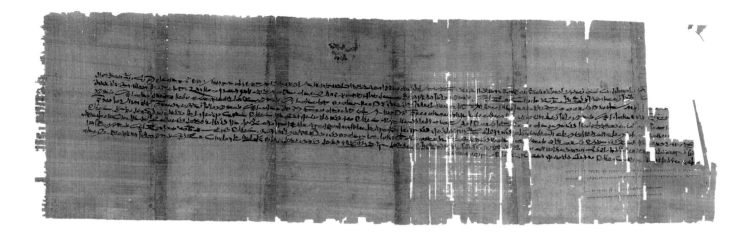

63. TRANSFER OF PROPERTY TO A WOMAN

Papyrus, ink
Ptolemaic period, reign of Ptolemy III, 9 March 239 B.C.
Faiyum, Hawara
Purchased in Cairo, 1932
L: 107.0; H: 33.5 cm
OIM 25263

Egyptian women could own land and participate in complex economic transactions. This contract is one of three made between the same man and woman, two of which involve ownership of one-third of a house and associated outbuilding. Two of the three documents are dated 9 March 239 B.C. One of these, now in Copenhagen (Papyrus Carlsberg 34),[1] is an annuity contract (for discussion of these contracts, see cat. no. 62) made by a man named Ankh-merwer[2] to the woman Her-ankh. Since annuity contracts are always or almost always made between husband and wife,[3] this should indicate that these two individuals were married.

The second of the documents dated to 239 B.C. (cat. no. 63) records that Ankh-merwer sold one-third of a two-story house and associated outbuilding to Her-ankh. Sales in Demotic texts involved two documents, the sale or transfer contract ("document concerning silver/money") and the "cession" document. The first document recorded the transfer of use of the property from party A to party B, but party A remained the legal owner of the property. The second document transferred actual legal ownership of the property from A to B. In case of an actual sale, both documents were written up at the same time. In the case of a lease or, especially, a mortgage, the transfer contract would be written but not the cession document.

This situation seems to be what is reflected in this case, since the third document (also now in Copenhagen, Papyrus Carlsberg 36[4]) between the two individuals is a cession document transferring actual legal ownership of the property; this cession document is dated between 17 July and 15 August 233 B.C., that is, six years after the transfer document. It would seem, then, that Ankh-merwer mortgaged his one-third share of the house and associated outbuilding to his wife and then, six years later, either defaulted on the mortgage and had to transfer legal ownership to his wife or for some other reason, perhaps as part of a divorce settlement, was forced to transfer the legal ownership. At the end of the annuity contract (P. Carlsberg 34), he agreed to abide not only by the legal obligations of that annuity contract but also the legal obligations of every document he has made for Her-ankh, including the Oriental Institute transfer document (cat. no. 63). In the Copenhagen cession document (P. Carlsberg 36) that transferred legal ownership to Her-ankh, Ankh-merwer noted Her-ankh's legal claim on him based on the transfer document (cat. no. 63). In addition, the brother and sister of Ankh-merwer (who might have some residual legal interest in this house and outbuilding which had been inherited through their common father) declared that they accepted the cession document and had no further legal claim on this property. They agreed that if anyone, in the future, came to claim the property in the name of their father or mother, they would help establish Her-ankh's legal title to the property. They also agreed not to hinder any future work Her-ankh might do on the property (whether building or tearing down).[5]

The situation is further complicated by references to another woman, Tay-iru, who seems to have had an interest in this house, or in the property belonging to Ankh-merwer in general. In both the Oriental Institute transfer document (cat. no. 63) and the annuity contract (P. Carlsberg 34), Tay-iru made a declaration at the end indicating that she had legal claim on Ankh-merwer because of legal documents which he had made to her. In the annuity contract she says, "Do everything above; my heart is satisfied." That is, she will not use her prior legal claim on Ankh-merwer to try to challenge or undermine this annuity contract. Similarly, Tay-iru consented to the transfer/mortgage contract, stating she had no further claim on the property "from today onward."

The documents do not make clear who Tay-iru was and how she was related to the parties to these three contracts, but one possible scenario is that Tay-iru was a previous wife of Ankh-merwer who had herself been given an annuity contract or other contract by Ankh-merwer. Since there is no reference in the annuity contract (P. Carlsberg 34) to Ankh-merwer's property serving as security for his pledge to support Her-ankh and no mention of their children inheriting his property, it is quite possible that his property was already pledged as the inheritance of children from the first marriage, to Tay-iru. The unusual omission in the annuity contract of the clause concerning children and the unusual consent clause at the end of the document, more at home in transfer documents, was noted by the editors.[6]

The property being transferred by Ankh-merwer to Her-ankh in the Oriental Institute document (cat. no. 63) is identified by giving the names of the owners, and inhabitants, of the houses or properties to the south, north, west, and east of the house and the outbuilding.[7] Her-ankh is said to be, now, the owner of the southern one-third of this house and outbuilding and no one, himself included, has the legal right to exercise control over this property from now on except her. Ankh-merwer swore that, if anyone tried to wrest the property from her, he would make them withdraw from their claim and clear every title deed for her. He also gave her all the documents (including those made to his father or his mother or to him) by which he gained legal title to the house and outbuilding since all the documents by which he gained ownership are now deemed to be legally hers. He agreed to take any oath in court which might be required to establish legal ownership. He specifically granted her the right to use the staircase to go to the roof and the right to go in and out of the "forehall, the main doorway, and the (other) exits of this aforesaid house." She is given specific permission to make repairs on her one-third of the house and the outbuilding. These rights are reconfirmed in the cession document by which legal ownership was transferred to Her-ankh.

Beneath the Demotic agreement there are two brief inscriptions written in Greek recording the deposit of the document in the official "chest" of the city of Crocodilopolis (capital of the Faiyum). These dockets thus record the official registration of this transfer of real property, as a result of which the relevant government agency had record of who owns the property and, equally importantly, is liable for taxes on it, now the woman Her-ankh. JHJ

NOTES

[1] Papyrus Copenhagen Hawara 1; published by Lüddeckens and Wasserman, *Demotische Urkunden*, pp. 2–11 and pl. 1.

[2] This is a different man named Ankh-merwer than the man who made Catalog No. 62. However, once again, most of the men mentioned in this document, both party A and the men related to him and the men related to party B, have the title God's Sealer and Embalmer; see above.

[3] See Johnson, "Annuity Contracts."

[4] P. Copenhagen Hawara 1; published by Lüddeckens and Wassermann, *Demotische Urkunden*, pp. 21–36 and pl. 3.

[5] If they or anyone in their name did hinder such work, they would have to pay a large monetary fine within five days and still remove themselves from the property.

[6] Lüddeckens and Wassermann, *Demotische Urkunden*, p. 11.

[7] All the men who own property adjacent to this house and outbuilding are again entitled God's Sealer and Embalmer (see above with note 2). It is worth noting that Ankh-merwer owned the house to the east of the house and to the south of the outbuilding while Her-ankh owned the building plot west of the outbuilding and north of Ankh-merwer's house. The property can be located within the city of Hawara by means of the indication that, to the east of the outbuilding which Her-ankh bought runs the "great street" and, across the street, the (wall, perhaps, of) the temple of Hawara. For a plan showing the suggested layout of the property involved, see Hughes and Jasnow, *Hawara Papyri*, p. 57; or Lüddeckdens and Wassermann, *Demotische Urkunden*, p. 35.

PUBLISHED

Hughes and Jasnow, *Hawara Papyri*, pp. 52–58, pls. 49–55.

64. STELA OF A MISTRESS OF THE HOUSE

Wood, gesso, pigment
Late Period, Dynasty 26, 664–525 B.C.
Luxor, Deir el-Bahri
Excavated by the Metropolitan Museum of Art, 1931
By Exchange with the Metropolitan Museum of Art, 1950
H: 37.5; W: 32.3; Th: 1.9 cm
OIM 18280

This stela was found as a part of the burial of the *nbt pr* ("mistress of the house") Diesenesyt. It shows the deceased before a table making offerings to Osiris, who is followed by Isis and the four sons of Horus. The lower registers contain a typical offering formula asking Osiris to provide the deceased with funerary offerings of bread, beer, cattle, birds, incense, wine, and milk.

Here, she is shown as an independent entity without any other members of her family represented. Her title *nbt pr* is probably more than merely a designation of being a married woman — it may indicate that she owned her own property. She is also shown as being able to present herself before the god and make offerings without the presence or assistance of a male relative.

Such a stela would not be economically possible for most ancient Egyptian women, but Diesenesyt came from an important and influential family. Her father was a prophet of Montu and her grandfather was the well-known vizier (like prime minister) Nespeqashuty. In fact, more is known about her than is known about Meresamun. However, based on Meresamun's titles, it is likely that she came from a similar, if not quite equal, social station.   JH

WOMEN AND THEIR EMPLOYMENT

Megaera Lorenz

As a temple singer, Meresamun held one of the few titled offices available to women at any period in Egyptian history. Men dominated the administrative and bureaucratic offices of both state and temple institutions and, hence, the historical record of ancient Egypt.

Women from wealthy and powerful families (as Meresamun almost certainly was) often held priestly positions, particularly as temple musicians. By far the most commonly held title for a woman by the New Kingdom was *nbt pr* "mistress of the house" or "owner of the house" — a title frequently and perhaps inappropriately translated as "housewife" (a decidedly modern and Western concept, and not particularly descriptive of what the title actually entailed). Some women held this title concurrently with a priestly title. However, these were hardly the only occupations available to women — nor were these occupations as simple as they seem at first glance.

A careful look at the evidence reveals that women of all classes were, in fact, a major presence in the functioning of Egyptian society and economy. Other women would have played a major part in a myriad of aspects of Meresamun's everyday life. She would have come into contact with women in the marketplace and with women who worked as servants in elite households (fig. 54).

FIGURE 54. Women are often portrayed as employees in elite households. Here, three musicians perform at a banquet. Their relatively low status is suggested by the lack of any reference to their personal names or their relationship to the family. The brief hieroglyphic texts are lyrics that praise Maat, Amun, and Ptah. Tomb of Rekhmire (Theban Tomb 100), Dynasty 18, ca. 1427 B.C. Photo: C. F. Nims

SOURCES AND PROBLEMS

The major problem with attempting to understand the work lives of women in ancient Egypt — especially women of low economic and social status — is that they are vastly underrepresented in historical sources. Even women who were wealthy or privileged enough to afford their own dedicatory monuments, such as statues or stelae, were most commonly depicted in relation to their husband or other male relatives.[1] The information that can be gleaned from archaeological sources is also limited. An excavated workshop, for example, may give many clues as to the nature of the work that took place there, but it reveals little about who was doing the work.

This is not to say that women's work is completely absent from the historical record. Egyptologists turn to two major sources when attempting to reconstruct the kinds of work that ancient Egyptian women engaged in: artistic representations (usually from funerary contexts) and private documents (such as letters, receipts, and legal documents).

Artistic representations from tombs are a particularly valuable source of information. In the Old Kingdom and Middle Kingdom, burials often included statues and models representing both men and women engaged in various types of work. Starting in the Old Kingdom and extending into the early New Kingdom, the walls of Egyptian private tomb chapels were frequently decorated with detailed scenes of "daily life," activities such as agricultural work, production of goods, musical performance, and dance. By the early Third Intermediate Period, when Meresamun lived, this type of tomb decoration had disappeared in favor of more ritualistic themes, such as vignettes from funerary texts like the Book of the Dead.[2] However, despite this temporal gap, the basic nature of the work depicted in the earlier tomb scenes — such as food and textile production — had probably not changed significantly by Meresamun's time.

Another problem with using tomb scenes to reconstruct daily life at any period in Egyptian history is that the content of the scenes is highly selective (they depict what the tomb owner — or at least the person responsible for funding the decoration of the tomb — chose to depict) and often formulaic. The information that they provide is fragmentary at best.

Private documents help fill in some of the gaps left by the more public and ritualistic artistic depictions found in funerary contexts. Letters, laundry lists, records of business transactions, and legal disputes all provide an invaluable glimpse into the daily lives of ancient Egyptian men and women. The information provided by these documents is also spotty, however — partially because those who were literate (probably a relatively small percentage of the population) are much better represented in written documents than those who were not. Another problem is that those documents that we have are often extant only through happy accidents of preservation, and thus certain time periods and geographic locations are much better represented than others.

WOMEN'S ROLE IN TEXTILE PRODUCTION

The role of Egyptian women in the production of textiles is attested as early as the Old Kingdom, although the first artistic representations of women engaged in textile manufacture date to the Middle Kingdom.[3] Several examples of women holding the title Overseer of the House of Weavers are known from the Old Kingdom. The Old Kingdom word for "weaver" was written simply as a seated woman holding a staff (once thought to be a weaver's shuttle), probably to be read ḥst "adorned one." This term may be a reference to the payments of costly jewelry that weavers often received in exchange for finished cloth, as depicted in a number of tomb paintings from the late Old Kingdom.[4] Several detailed artistic representations of textile production are known from the Middle Kingdom, from tomb paintings and models. At this time, if the artistic representations are to be trusted, women had a monopoly on all aspects of linen textile manufacture, including the harvesting of the flax.[5] A detailed scene from the tomb of Khnumhotep at Beni Hasan depicts a group of women in a weaving workshop engaging in various stages of the textile production process (fig. 55). On the left, two women weave a length of cloth on a horizontal loom (the loom appears to be standing upright, but this is due to an Egyptian artistic convention in which objects were drawn from the most recognizable angle, without regard to perspective). A looped fringe is visible on the left side of the finished portion of cloth at the bottom of the loom. This type of fringe, called a weft or selvedge fringe, is characteristic of pharaonic textiles woven on horizontal looms.[6] Catalog No. 65

FIGURE 55. Women weave and spin thread in a weavers' workshop. Facsimile by Norman de Garis Davies of a painting from the tomb of Khnumhotep at Beni Hasan. Dynasty 12, ca. 1877–1870 B.C. Rogers Fund 1933, 33.8.16. Image copyright the Metropolitan Museum of Art

exhibits an excellent example of a weft fringe in which the loops of the fringe have been cut open to form long tassels. A female overseer observes the weavers' work. Her advanced age and status are indicated by her large breasts and rolls of fat.

To the right of the weavers, two women are engaged in the production of thread. One woman kneels, facing right, as she rolls flax fibers into loose thread. A ball of this unfinished thread sits in front of her, ready to be placed in a spinning bowl (cat. no. 70). These bowls probably contained water, which helped keep the fibers cohesive and improved the tension of the thread during the spinning process. The thread was secured to a loop built into the bottom of the bowl.[7] An adolescent girl stands at the far right of the scene, facing the woman roving the flax. She spins thread from both of the bowls with two drop spindles. She grasps one spindle by the rod in her left hand and rolls it along the back of her thigh to begin the twist before allowing the spindle to drop and spin. A second spindle dangles from her right hand. This spindle has a discoid whorl at the top, very much like Catalog No. 68.

In addition to the numerous artistic representations of weaving dating to the Middle Kingdom, there are a handful of intriguing textual references to the role of women in the textile industry. A particularly interesting letter found at the Middle Kingdom settlement at Kahun, dating to the late Twelfth Dynasty, describes a strike among female weavers who had not been paid for their services. The letter is from a nbt pr ("mistress of the house") named Irer to an unnamed superior. Irer informed her addressee that she could not deal with the issue herself because she was busy with duties in the temple. Meanwhile, the weavers were "left abandoned, thinking they wouldn't get food provisions inasmuch as not any news of you has been heard." She goes on to tell him that he "should spend some time here since [not] any clothes [have been made] while my attention is being directed to the temple, and the warp-threads are set up on the loom without it being possible to weave them."[8] These women were probably employed either by one of the local temples or by the private estate of one of the elite citizens of the town.

Unfortunately, the evidence from the New Kingdom is more limited. There are only three known New Kingdom artistic depictions of textile production, and again, these come from funerary contexts, specifically, scenes from Theban private tombs.[9] All three of these images depict mostly male weavers, using upright rather than horizontal looms. These factors suggest that major changes took place in the textile industry with the advent of the New Kingdom, most significantly that a previously female-dominated industry had fallen into the purview of men.

However, despite the fact that men were clearly more heavily involved in textile production in the New Kingdom than they had been previously, a closer examination of the evidence reveals that women were still very much involved in the industry as well. The tomb of Neferrenpet (Theban Tomb 133), the chief of weavers in the mortuary temple of Ramesses II (Dynasty 19), depicts weavers in the workshop that Neferrenpet supervised. One of the five weavers depicted is a woman (fig. 56).

Textual evidence from the New Kingdom demonstrates that women also continued to produce cloth on a smaller scale, both for personal use and for barter. One particularly intriguing document, a record of a court case dating to the reign of Ramesses II, describes a situation in which a woman used several textiles that she herself had apparently produced as part of the payment in the purchase of a female servant. The cloth items are listed in her testimony along with their equivalent value in silver.[10] A handful of texts from the workmen's village at Deir el-Medina make reference to the wives of workmen supplementing their personal income by weaving and bartering cloth.[11] A legal document from the same village, dating to the late Nineteenth Dynasty, lists a long series of charges against the chief workman Paneb, one among them being that he had forced the wives of several of the workers in his charge to weave clothing for him (apparently without compensation).[12]

Preserved textiles demonstrate that the use of the horizontal loom continued well beyond the end of the Middle Kingdom, despite its absence from New Kingdom artistic representations. The textile on display in this exhibit (cat. no. 65) has the selvedge fringe characteristic of cloth woven on a horizontal loom, although the cloth probably dates to the New Kingdom. The selvedge fringe is also found on textiles that can be dated with certainty to the Third Intermediate Period and later.[13]

Although there is, unfortunately, very little evidence regarding the production of textiles in the Third Intermediate Period itself, there is no reason to assume that the situation had changed drastically from that of the New Kingdom. Women very likely continued to participate actively in textile production both at the home industry level and on a larger scale. Textual evidence from the Ptolemaic period reveals that women found employment as weavers (alongside men) long after the end of the Third Intermediate Period.[14]

New Kingdom evidence shows that weaving workshops were often attached to wealthy private estates and to temples. Meresamun may have encountered female weavers who were staffed by the temple that employed

FIGURE 56. Men and women work in the weavers' workshop attached to the mortuary temple of Ramesses II. Scene from the tomb of Neferrenpet (Theban Tomb 133). Dynasty 19, ca. 1279–1213 B.C. Courtesy of the Egypt Exploration Society

her, or even had a staff of weavers attached to her own private estate. Meresamun herself probably never put her hand to the loom. Throughout most of Egyptian history, weaving seems to have been an occupation of women of lower economic and social status than most temple singers. In fact, a late Middle Kingdom text (known to modern scholars as the Admonitions of Ipuwer) describes the deplorable idea of a temple musician forced to resort to weaving: "There are no remedies for it; noblewomen suffer like maidservants, minstrels are at the looms within the weaving-rooms, and what they sing to the Songstress-goddess is mourning."[15]

WOMEN AND FOOD PRODUCTION

There is evidence for women's involvement in the production of bread and beer — the staples of the ancient Egyptian diet — throughout the entire pharaonic period. They participated in almost every stage of the food production process, from assisting with the harvest to cooking and brewing. While men and women seem to have participated equally in certain tasks related to food production, some tasks (such as the grinding of grain) were specifically the domain of women.[16]

Men were responsible for most aspects of brewing, but women were frequently depicted straining the chaffy residue that was created in the brewing process.[17] The most common depictions of this process show women pushing beer mash through a large, basket-like sieve into a pottery vessel. Catalog No. 72 also seems to depict a woman straining beer, although she uses a very small bowl or sieve rather than the usual large basket-like strainer.

Baking and brewing were popular subjects in funerary art at most periods. Many Old and Middle

Kingdom tombs contained "servant statues," like the two examples in the present exhibit (cat. nos. 71–72), which depict people engaged in various types of work. These statues allowed the deceased to magically benefit from the tasks being portrayed. While most of these statues were uninscribed and are often assumed to represent anonymous servant figures, a few of them, such as Catalog Nos. 71–72, are inscribed with personal names and even specify the relationships of these individuals to the owner of the tomb. However, it is unlikely that the children of a wealthy official, like the two women represented in this exhibit, would have regularly engaged in food production activities. The statues may have had the more symbolic function of showing the tomb owner's dependents providing support to their benefactor in the afterlife while also allowing them to benefit from his funerary cult. In any case, typically servants attached to the estate of a wealthy official (rather than family members) were responsible for supplying the household with food and drink.[18]

A scene from an early Middle Kingdom tomb at Thebes (Theban Tomb 366) depicts a more realistic scenario than that represented by statues of the tomb owner's children engaged in menial tasks. The scene, which is located close to the depiction of the funerary procession, shows a group of female servants engaging in food preparation (fig. 57). The scene is unusual in that these women are identified by name, along with the title "servant." Presumably, they were employees of the tomb owner who worked either for his personal estate or for the king's "harem" (or private apartments), where the tomb owner himself was employed.[19]

In the New Kingdom, women were still active in the production of food and beer, for personal use and in service to others (e.g., relatives or employers). In a letter from Deir el-Medina, a woman tells her sister that

FIGURE 57. Five female servants prepare food. Painting from the tomb of Djari at Thebes (Theban Tomb 366). Dynasty 11, ca. 2055–1985 B.C. The Metropolitan Museum of Art, Rogers Fund, 1931 (31.6.1). Image copyright the Metropolitan Museum of Art

she is sending barley, "and you shall have it ground for me and add emmer to it. And you shall make me bread with it, for I have been quarreling with Merymaat (my husband)."[20] She goes on to explain that her husband's specific complaint is that her family is not providing for them, "whereas all people furnish bread, beer, and fish daily [to] their (family) members."

Meresamun, being a wealthy and high-ranking individual, probably had a staff of cooks and brewers attached to her personal estate. There must have been a large staff responsible for the preparation of food provisions for the temple where she was employed, as well. However, these were not the only venues in which she would have encountered female workers during her daily routine. Women were active participants in the thriving pharaonic barter economy and were also employed by the state to receive, distribute, and process goods.

WOMEN IN THE MARKETPLACE

The ancient Egyptian economy was based on barter, exchange, and redistribution of wealth. Currency did not yet exist in Egypt as of Meresamun's time, although goods were often assigned values based on a system of precious metal weights and measures (see, for example, Papyrus Cairo 65739, discussed above). A working person's salary would have consisted of goods

(food, clothing, and raw materials) and services (people employed by the state were sometimes provided with servants, who were in turn paid by the government).[21] However, people could and did supplement their incomes by engaging in private trade, and women were active participants in the marketplace from the Old Kingdom on.

The earliest evidence for women engaging in barter in a market setting dates to the Fifth and Sixth Dynasties. Several relief fragments from Saqqara dating to this period depict women as both vendors and buyers.[22]

There is a great deal of tantalizing evidence for the role of women in the marketplace during the New Kingdom. A lively scene — now lost — from the late Eighteenth Dynasty tomb of Kenamun depicts Syrian trading ships docking at a marketplace in Thebes (fig. 58).[23] Three vendors are shown manning booths on the dock, and one of these is a woman. Her goods include textiles and sandals, among other items more difficult to identify.

A particularly fascinating but enigmatic scene from the lost Theban Tomb A4 depicts what appears to be a marketplace in which large numbers of women transport, arrange, and possibly barter a variety of foodstuffs with the supervision and assistance of a few men. A large group of women are depicted clapping, singing, and dancing, led by two women with tambourines, on

FIGURE 58. Male and female vendors operate sales booths on a Theban dockside. Scene from the tomb of Kenamun at Thebes (Theban Tomb 162). Dynasty 18, ca. 1400 B.C. Photo: Oriental Institute

the left side of the bottom register.[24] Interestingly, the text that accompanies the scene suggests that these goods are being distributed to the people of Thebes as a gesture of beneficence from the king. The text above the rejoicing women states that "the people of Thebes are in jubilation," and another caption in the lowest register explains that the figures depicted there are "taking fish to the people of Thebes in their houses out of the food catch of the ruler." A caption in the top register states that the goods that are being brought to the denizens of Thebes are from "the goods from vile Kush which his Majesty brought from...."[25] Whether they are bartering the goods or simply distributing them, the women involved in this scene appear to be employees of the state rather than private vendors.

The scene from Theban Tomb A4 may be an artistic representation of a practice known from written records at Deir el-Medina, in which people were employed by the state to receive and process wages for the denizens of the village. This form of employment was probably compulsory, but the state-employed servants were salaried — although men were paid considerably more than women for their services.[26]

Several letters from Deir el-Medina also provide information about the role of women in the marketplace. Many of these letters describe situations in which women were asked to make a purchase by a third party (who would typically provide the capital necessary for the trade). Both men and women could send female agents to make purchases for them. For example, in Ostracon Deir el-Medina 116, a woman has been asked by a man — possibly her employer — to trade some wool for copper pieces. She writes to him asking for additional supplies to make the purchase. The vendor of the copper pieces is also female.[27] In Ostracon Deir el-Medina 117, a woman asks another woman to purchase a tunic for her in exchange for a bracelet.[28] Men were also frequently sent on such errands, so the task of haggling on behalf of an employer or relative was not gender restricted.

UNSUNG SINGERS: WOMEN AND THE ADMINISTRATION OF THE TEMPLE INSTITUTION

While Meresamun's title implies simply that she participated in the ritual aspects of the cult of Amun as a priestly musician, a few tantalizing private letters to and from other temple singers suggest that she may also have been heavily involved in the administration of the temple.

A fascinating Theban letter dating to the Twentieth Dynasty from a singer of Amun named Henuttawy to a necropolis scribe sheds light on some of the priestess' non-cultic duties. Henuttawy complains that she had checked a recent shipment of grain to the temple and found it short. She has decided to let that particular oversight pass, but she sternly instructs her addressee to be more careful with the next shipment:

> See, you shall join up with Paseny, and you two shall consult with the overseer of granaries concerning the grain for Amun, United with Eternity, because he (Amun) hasn't got even one *oipe*-measure's worth for his divine offerings today. You mustn't abandon him, either of you two.[29]

In a letter of the same provenance and time period, another singer of Amun named Mutenope receives orders from the necropolis scribe Nesamenope to carry out a variety of administrative tasks.[30] These tasks include dispatching a courier to deliver a land title to another priest and provide fruit crops for the plot of land in question; delegating workers to clear the land and prepare it for planting; and paying a weaponsmith.

Letters like these demonstrate that the job of a temple singer went much further than its ritual aspects. Meresamun may have been required not only to propitiate the god, but also to manage much of the day-to-day business of the temple. In the course of carrying out her duties, she would have interacted with other working women on a regular basis. She may have overseen other women who were employed to produce cloth and process foodstuffs for the temple, or commissioned women in her employ to obtain goods through barter in the marketplace. As a wealthy woman, she probably employed women in her own household to provide goods and services for her personal use. Meresamun was a member of a society in which women played an active and important role in the workforce, despite their misleading silence in the historical record.

NOTES

[1] Roehrig, "Women's Work," p. 13.
[2] Ikram and Dodson, *Mummy in Ancient Egypt*, pp. 22–45.
[3] Roehrig, "Women's Work," p. 19.
[4] Fischer, *Egyptian Women*, pp. 20–21.
[5] Roehrig, "Women's Work," p. 19.
[6] Vogelsang-Eastwood, "Textiles," p. 277.

7 Barber, "Women's Work," p. 192.

8 Papyrus Kahun III.3, translated in Wente, *Letters*, pp. 82–83.

9 Roehrig, "Women's Work," p. 21.

10 Papyrus Cairo 65739, published in Gardiner, "Lawsuit."

11 Toivari-Viitala, *Women at Deir el-Medina*, pp. 233–34.

12 Papyrus Salt 124, published in Černý, "Papyrus Salt 124."

13 Compare catalog no. 48 in van Rooij and Vogelsang-Eastwood, "Pharaonic Textiles," p. 50, pl. 3.

14 See, for example, PSI IV 341 and PSI VI 599 (early third century A.D.), published in Rowlandson, ed., *Women and Society*, pp. 265–66.

15 Faulkner, "Admonitions," p. 55.

16 Roehrig, "Women's Work," p. 14.

17 Roehrig, "Women's Work," p. 15. See also several examples described in Breasted, *Egyptian Servant Statues*, pp. 30–35, pls. 29b, 30a–b, 31a–b, and 32b.

18 Roth, "Meaning of Menial Labor," pp. 116–17.

19 Roehrig, "Women's Work," pp. 14–15. See also Porter and Moss, *Topographical Bibliography*, vol 1, part 1, pp. 429–30.

20 O. Prague 1826, published in Wente, *Letters*, pp. 147–48.

21 Toivari-Viitala, *Women at Deir el-Medina*, pp. 5–6.

22 Fischer, *Egyptian Women*, pp. 22–23.

23 Davies and Faulkner, "Syrian Trading Venture."

24 Manniche, *Lost Tombs*, pl. 7.

25 Manniche, *Lost Tombs*, pp. 65–66.

26 Toivari-Viitali, *Women at Deir el-Medina*, pp. 5–6.

27 Translated in Wente, *Letters*, p. 156.

28 Wente, *Letters*, p. 156.

29 Late Ramesside Letter 37, translated in Wente, *Letters*, pp. 174–75.

30 Late Ramesside Letter 36, in Wente, *Letters*, pp. 175–76.

65. TEXTILE

Linen
New Kingdom(?), second millennium B.C.
Purchased in Luxor, 1932
L: 53; W: 45 cm
OIM 16899

This sheet of cloth was purchased on the antiquities market as part of an "embalmer's outfit." It is described in the original registration file as an embalmer's sheet, but without the original contextual information, it is difficult to say precisely how it was used.

The sheet is an undecorated, rectangular piece of linen, off-white in color with several patches of yellow and brown discoloration. The cloth was at one time tightly folded and is still heavily creased along the lines of folding. Three of the edges are completely unfinished, suggesting that the sheet was cut from a larger piece of cloth (possibly by a modern antiquities

65, detail

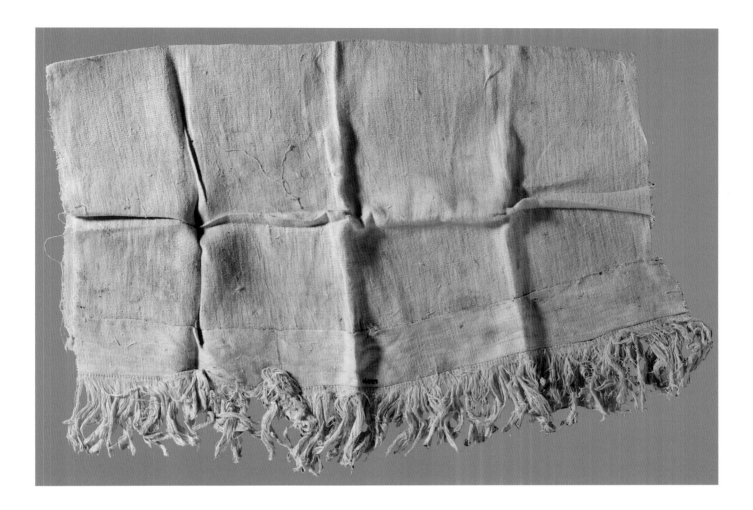

dealer). One of the short edges has been modified with a sewn-on strip with a selvedge edge (the closed-off longitudinal edge of a woven cloth) and weft fringe. The threads of the fringe probably originally formed loops, which were cut to create tassels.[1] The fringed strip was clearly cut from a different piece of cloth than the rest of the sheet, as the weave of the strip is much tighter than that of the main body of the sheet. Both pieces of cloth are warp-faced, meaning that the density of warp threads (the threads that are stretched lengthwise across the loom) is higher than that of weft threads (threads that are woven across the loom horizontally). The type of weave in both pieces is a tabby or simple weave, in which single weft threads are woven alternately over and under single warp threads.

The warp-faced tabby weave and the presence of a selvedge fringe are characteristic of pharaonic textiles of all periods. The selvedge fringe indicates that the cloth was woven on a horizontal ground loom, the type always depicted in Middle Kingdom artistic representations of looms. Although artistic representations of weaving from the New Kingdom onward typically depict vertical looms, preserved textiles show that the use of horizontal looms continued into Meresamun's time and beyond.[2] ML

NOTES

[1] Van Rooij and Vogelsang-Eastwood, "Pharaonic Textiles," p. 19; and compare Catalog No. 48.

[2] Van Rooij and Vogelsang-Eastwood, "Pharaonic Textiles," p. 19.

Spinning Equipment

Hand-held spindles were an essential component in the production of textiles in ancient Egypt. The spindle is used to create fine thread by twisting together moistened lengths of loose fiber. Ancient Egyptian weavers used spindles to create the fine flax thread that went into the production of linen cloth.

Spindle whorls were used as weights to produce tension in the thread and keep the spindle spinning, twisting the fibers together to form a tight, sturdy thread. Ancient Egyptian spindles typically had the whorl located at the top of the spindle rod.[1] A groove cut into the end of the spindle rod above the whorl would hold the thread in place and guide the direction of the spin.[2]

As these examples demonstrate, whorls were made in a wide variety of materials and shapes. Convex, dome-shaped whorls, like Catalog Nos. 66 and 67, were typical of the New Kingdom, although they begin to appear as early as the late Middle Kingdom.[3] The convex side of the whorl faced the top of the spindle. Catalog No. 67 is the smallest of the whorls represented in this exhibit and is made of highly polished white stone, probably calcite. Because of its fine workmanship, this object was mistakenly classified as an "ornament" in the original accession list. The spindle rod would have been inserted through the drilled hole in the center of the whorl.

Much of the original spindle rod of Catalog No. 69 is still preserved. Although the date of this spindle is very late (probably early to mid-third century A.D.) and its provenance is Nubian rather than Egyptian, it is similar to the types of spindles that would have been in use in Egypt during Meresamun's time. A metal nail is wedged into the drill-hole in the center of the whorl alongside the spindle, and it protrudes in a hook beyond the top of the whorl. The hook was used to help hold the thread in place during spinning, like the grooves used in older Egyptian spindles. This example is one of several excavated from a Meroitic cemetery in Ballana, Nubia. This spindle, along with several other spindle whorls, was part of the burial equipment of a woman. The presence of spindles and whorls in the burials of several women at the cemetery suggests that cloth production was an important part of their life.

Catalog Nos. 66 and 68 are both made of fired clay. Catalog No. 66 is made of coarse clay and is roughly decorated on one side with incised grooves. Such decoration is not uncommon on Egyptian spindle whorls

and may have served as a mark to identify the spindle with a particular owner.[4] The shape of this whorl is unusual, as there is no flat side. Between its atypical shape and the lack of contextual information, it is very difficult to date this whorl.

Catalog No. 68 is made of much finer-grained clay than Catalog No. 66 and has a red slip on one side. It is discoid (flat on both sides), a shape typical of earlier Egyptian spindles. Flat whorls like this one were in use from prehistoric times into the late Middle Kingdom.[5] ML

NOTES

[1] Vogelsang-Eastwood, "Textiles," p. 272.
[2] Barber, *Women's Work*, p. 193, fig. 8.3.
[3] Vogelsang-Eastwood, "Textiles," p. 272.
[4] Vogelsang-Eastwood, "Textiles," p. 272.
[5] Vogelsang-Eastwood, "Textiles," p. 272.

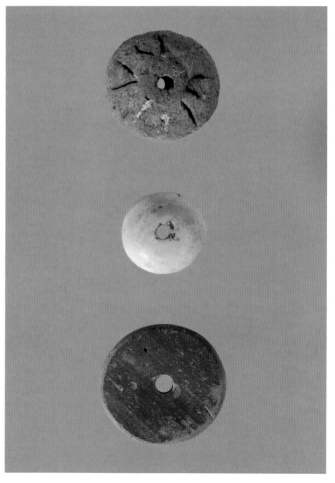

66

67

68

66. SPINDLE WHORL

Pottery
Unknown
Gift from the collection of James H. Breasted, 1936
D: 3.2; Th: 1.2 cm
OIM 17112

67. SPINDLE WHORL

White stone (calcite?)
New Kingdom(?), 2nd millennium B.C.
Purchased in Egypt, Mallawi, 1894–1895
D: 2.4; Th: .6.0 cm
OIM 569

68. SPINDLE WHORL

Pottery
Pre-New Kingdom, 2nd millennium B.C.
Gift from the collection of James H. Breasted, 1936
D: 3.7; H: .4.0 cm
OIM 17113

69. SPINDLE

Wood, metal (copper?)
Meroitic, 3rd century A.D.
Nubia, Ballana, tomb B58E
Excavated by the Oriental Institute Nubian Expedition, 1963–1964
Whorl D: 4.3 cm; Distaff L: 16.5 cm
OIM 22527c

PUBLISHED

Williams, *Meroitic Remains from Qustul Cemetery Q*, vol. 1, p. 159; vol. 2, pl. 90c.

70. SPINNING BOWL

Baked clay
Byzantine period, ca. A.D. 600
Luxor, Monastery of Epiphanius
Excavated by the Metropolitan Museum of Art, 1914
By Exchange with the Metropolitan Museum of Art, 1968
OIM 27369

The Egyptians used spinning bowls in the production of thread from prehistoric times until well beyond the end of the pharaonic period. Spinning bowls were used to hold loose fibers as they were being spun into thread. The loop in the bowl was used to secure the thread during spinning. The bowl may have been filled with water to dampen the flax fibers, which helped create a smooth, fine thread. While the bowls were usually made of fired clay, like this example, they were occasionally made of stone.   ML

Servant Statues

Although these two statues date to the Old Kingdom and probably served a very specific ritual or cultic function, they depict activities that remained largely unchanged throughout much of Egyptian history: the preparation of bread and beer. As a high-status individual, Meresamun probably employed servants who prepared food for her household, or even oversaw some of the food production that took place in the temple where she was employed.

These statues came from the tomb of an Old Kingdom official named Nikauinpu, who probably lived during the Fifth Dynasty. The statues were meant to represent individuals (specifically, members of the tomb-owner's family) rather than anonymous servants of the dead. Although service to the tomb owner was part of their function, they may also have been intended to allow the tomb owner's dependents to share in the benefits of his funerary cult.[1] The activities represented by these two statues are grain milling (a task that was apparently exclusive to women at all periods of pharaonic history) and the straining of beer mash.   ML

NOTE

[1] Roth, "Meaning of Menial Labor," pp. 106–09.

71. STATUE OF WOMAN GRINDING GRAIN

Limestone, pigment
Old Kingdom, Dynasty 5, probably reign of Niuserre, ca. 2445–2414 B.C.
Probably from Giza
Purchased in Cairo, 1920
H: 20.5; W: 11.5; L: 31.1 cm
OIM 10622

This statue depicts one of the tomb owner's daughters, Nebet-em-pet, grinding grain on a large palette. She kneels and leans forward, her right foot crossed over her left heel. She grasps a grinding stone in both hands and pushes it forward across the palette. There is a pile of grain at the near end of the palette, between her knees. Like most of the statues in the group, she looks up from her task and gazes ahead. Her head is covered in a white cap with a red band, which is tucked behind her ears, and her hair is not visible. She wears a simple skirt that goes from waist to knees. Her skin is painted yellow, the color traditionally used in depictions of ancient Egyptian women, and there are still traces of black pigment around her eyes. Traces of black around her wrists may indicate bracelets. Her name is inscribed beside her right knee.

The palette that she is using to grind the grain is known as a "saddle quern," a type of grain-milling technology that was widely used before the invention of the rotary quern in the fifth to third centuries B.C.[1] Such querns can produce very fine flour, which was used to bake the bread that was one of the major staples of Egyptian life during all periods.　ML

NOTE

[1] Samuel, "Brewing and Baking," p. 560.

72. STATUE OF WOMAN MASHING BEER

Limestone, pigment
Old Kingdom, Dynasty 5, probably reign of Niuserre, ca. 2445–2414 B.C.
Probably from Giza
Purchased in Cairo, 1920
H: 30.5; W: 11.7; L: 21.1 cm
OIM 10635

This statue represents another daughter of Nikauinpu named Merit. She stands over a large pottery vat filled with liquid, probably beer. With her right hand, she dips a bowl or sieve into the liquid, while she steadies herself by grasping the edge of the vat with her left hand. Her left shoulder is higher than her right, indicating the motion of leaning to the right as she dips the sieve. The beer vat is supported on four lumps. The supports are painted the same shade of red as the vat, suggesting that they are also made of pottery.

Like Nebet-em-pet (cat. no. 71), the woman depicted here wears a cap, but her hair is visible beneath it. Her hair is incised to represent the texture of curls or plaits. She wears a skirt that extends from below her breasts to just above her knees. Her skin is painted the traditional yellow, and her lips are pigmented pink, adding a naturalistic quality to the face. Her gaze is fixed ahead.

There are two inscriptions on the statue base, but only one of them (on her right side, giving her name and filiation) appears to be complete.

Ancient Egyptian beer was brewed from coarsely ground grain that was high in chaff, so the beer had to be sieved during the brewing process to remove the unwanted chaffy residue.[1] That stage in the process is probably what is represented by this statue.　ML

NOTE

[1] Samuel, "Brewing and Baking," p. 554.

PUBLISHED (SELECTED)

Breasted (Jr.), *Egyptian Servant Statues*; Roth, "Meaning of Menial Labor," pp. 103–21, no. 7; Teeter, *Ancient Egypt*, no. 7.

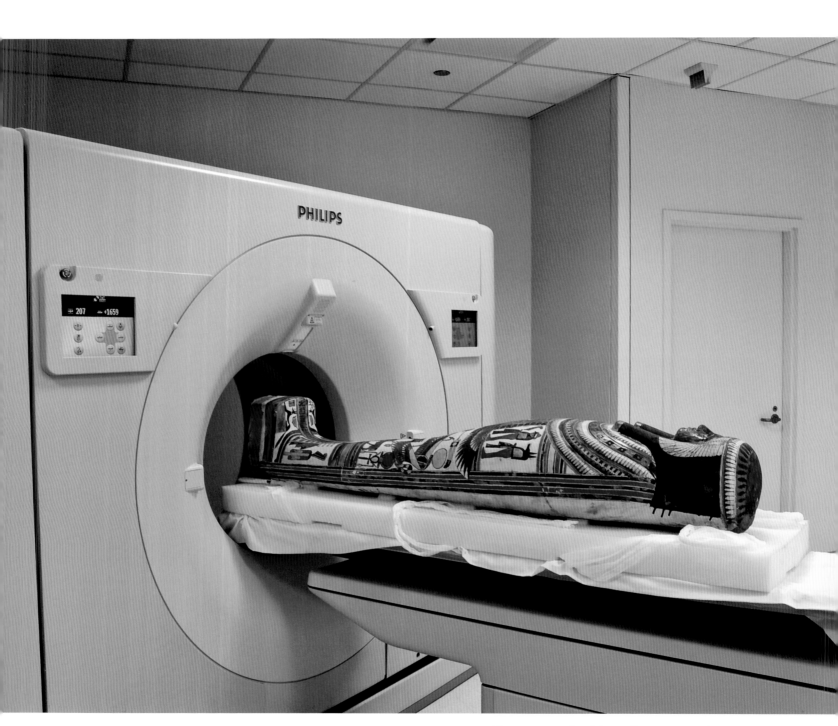

FIGURE 59. The mummy on the Philips Brilliance iCT 256-slice scanner

CT SCANNING OF MERESAMUN

MICHAEL VANNIER, M.D.

The mummy and coffin of Meresamun were scanned twice in 2008; once in July and again in September. We used a 64-channel CT scanner in July and a brand new 256-channel scanner in September. Most of the previously published studies of mummies using CT scanning employed sixteen or fewer channels. The image quality is related to a significant degree to the number of channels. Advances in imaging technology and computers made it possible to increase the number of channels recently.

SOME CT SCAN OBSERVATIONS

The tens of thousands of images we acquired this year exhaustively sampled the coffin and its contents (figs. 59–77). These data are archived in digital form, so they can be reused and evaluated using post-processing image analysis and computer graphics tools.

To date, we have evaluated the data sets using the *Philips Brilliance Workstation* software and post-processing tools. *Osirix* software on the *Apple Macintosh* has been used as well. We were able to make many new observations that were not made when the mummy was first scanned in 1991.

We found that the body was mummified in the usual manner (see cat. no. 1) with many post-mortem changes. Most striking is desiccation of the soft tissues. Lacking any moisture, the body was wrapped in many layers of linen. Some of the body wrappings are particularly thick and dense, compatible with a textile shroud impregnated with radiodense material, perhaps as a moisture barrier. The body is situated asymmetrically in the coffin, which appears to be of a single unit laminated construction decorated with mineral pigments and bound with sinew in the dorsal midline.

The skeleton is exceptionally well preserved. The bones belong to a young female, perhaps late 20s to mid-30s in age. The pelvis is gynecoid, without convincing evidence of childbearing. Almost no degenerative changes are seen anywhere in the skeleton, and the bone density/thickness is normal. There is no evidence of pre-mortem bony trauma, even minor.

The individual is symmetric, well proportioned, and without scoliosis or anomalies.

We did find several surprising features of this mummy. First, the teeth are severely worn at the occlusal surfaces (where they meet when biting). The wear on all the teeth is far greater than we ever see in modern humans. Second, there are two and perhaps more ornamental objects (amulets?) in the coffin. There appears to be an extra spinal vertebral segment in the cervicothoracic spine. This individual had an elongated neck and very symmetric face with well-developed sinuses and wide-set eyes. We cannot discern breast features or hair, probably due to desiccation and post-mortem processing. We can see the symmetric external earlobes and a small anterior overbite. Remarkably, all the teeth are present, including the wisdom teeth (3rd molars). No evidence of tooth decay or periodontal disease (the principal cause of tooth loss in modern humans) was found.

We found numerous fractures and fissures in the skin and several bones. All these are clearly post-mortem changes, but are somewhat difficult to explain. It takes a great deal of force to fracture the spine, collarbone, and upper ribs. Despite the presence of these fractures, the alignment of the skeleton is normal and they are nondisplaced. Some of the fractures or fissures are limited to the soft tissues (e.g., skin and subcutaneous tissues), so they may be related to long-term effects of drying. It is unclear whether the upper spine fractures took place near the time of death, but several of the fractures are clearly post-mortem since they extend into the packing material inserted into the thorax (for example).

Innumerable additional anatomic findings have already been made, and we expect that continuing re-evaluation of the CT datasets will yield further information. Having archived all the images, we can go back again and again as questions arise to reprocess the data sets and uncover new findings. One of the most important and exciting aspects of the CT studies is the fact that we now have access to exceedingly detailed high-quality information on the coffin and its contents. Collecting the data is complete, but the analysis may continue as insights and experience guide our further investigation of the mummy.

A Note on the Philips iCT 256-Channel CT Scanner

A new spiral CT scanner with 128 detector rows and 256 channels that provides 8 cm of coverage per rotation was installed near the Emergency Department. This unit, the Philips iCT (where i stands for intelligent) has exceptional specifications, such as 250 msec rotation time, very high generator output and tube heating capacity, with up to 100 slice per second reconstruction to provide exquisite images in 2D, 3D, and 4D. This unit has recently completed beta testing and has been certified for routine clinical use, with special capabilities that meet the most demanding requirements of cardiopulmonary, vascular, pediatric, neuroimaging, and abdominopelvic examinations. There are obvious benefits of this fast scanner for freezing motion when patients are unable to cooperate with breathholding, in CT perfusion dynamic contrast enhancement, x-ray dose reduction, and for arterial bolus examinations. We are among the first in the world to install this scanner and are using it to expand our CT examination portfolio.

The characteristics of this state-of-the-art CT scanner that make it particularly valuable for the Meresamun examination are exceptionally high image quality due to denser sampling, low noise, and the incorporation of recent advances in image reconstruction algorithms as well as detector construction with scatter reduction. The exceptional image quality is significantly better than prior generation CT scanners. To our knowledge, no other mummy has been studied using a 256-slice CT scanner.

FIGURE 60. The entire coffin was included in the scan yielding a volume of approximately 19.5 liters or 5.15 gallons. This volume is roughly one-half of a modern coffin for a small adult, reflecting medium stature by today's standards as well as contraction of body girth by the removal of fat and moisture. We know that the mummy remains in a relatively low moisture state since the CT scan x-ray attenuation values for the non-bony contents are very low (e.g., negative Hounsfield units, a relative scale based on water with a value of zero). To measure negative on this scale, the mummy must contain mostly air and very little water

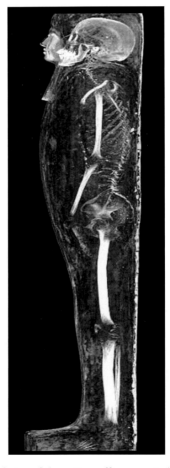

FIGURE 61. Lateral view of the entire coffin generated from 1,500 CT scan slices. The legs are extended in a standing position, but the posture is not fully erect, especially at the neck. A large amount of packing material is present behind the neck. The feet are not visible, since the coffin is relatively more dense at that region. The back of the coffin is very flat and it has a higher overall density than the front

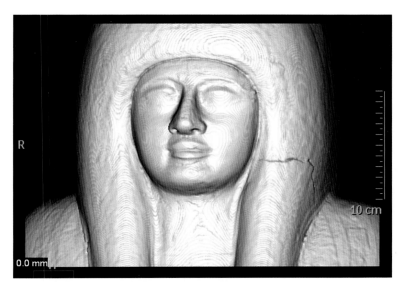

FIGURE 62. The external surface of the coffin was evaluated with CT revealing asymmetries in the eyes, nose, and slightly opened mouth. Careful inspection shows that the eyes are not bilaterally symmetric and the lips are parted more on the right than the left. There is an obvious crack in the coffin at the right of this image. This crack has not propagated further and may be due to a direct blow at this location, sometime in the past three millennia

FIGURE 63. Asymmetries in the eyes, nose, and mouth are clearly seen in this magnified surface view of the coffin. There is a very subtle defect in the left cheek (dark horizontal line), which corresponds to underlying post-mortem fractures, found with CT scanning, in the jaw and near the cervical spine and thoracic inlet. All these fractures are probably related and may have occurred simultaneously if the coffin was dropped. The surface imperfection in the cheek may be due to the fracture line in the headdress seen in figure 62

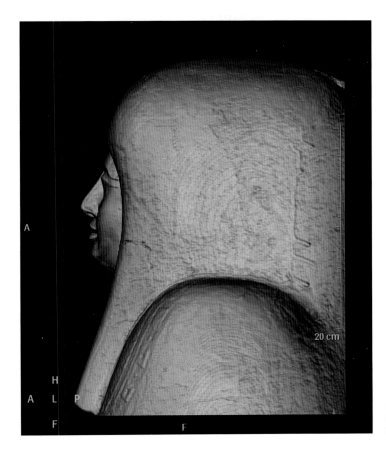

FIGURE 64. This lateral view of the coffin shows the non-displaced surface crack, prominent shoulders and headdress, short forehead, and a line of dried paint drips near the very flat posterior surface

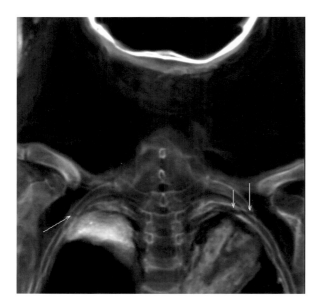

FIGURE 65. Coronal slab view of the upper chest and lower neck shows packing material in the superior recesses of the chest cavity where the lungs had been. Arrows indicate the presence of subtle transverse non-displaced post-mortem fractures. In general, the skeleton is well mineralized with minimal degenerative changes of aging

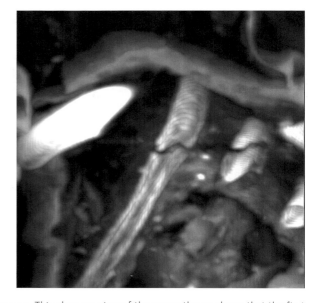

FIGURE 66. This close-up view of the upper thorax shows that the first and second ribs are fractured, but not displaced. The fracture line runs horizontally through the central part of this image as a subtle dark irregular contour which involves bone and the packing material that fills the thoracic cavity. This and numerous other subtle fractures were found with the 64- and 256-slice CT scanners, but were not previously detected. Their orientation approximates the surface crack in the coffin

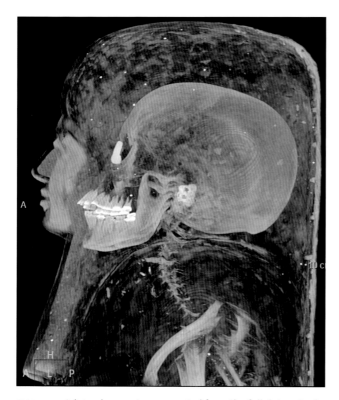

FIGURE 67. A lateral x-ray view generated from the full data sets shows both the coffin and skeleton simultaneously. The exaggerated cervical lordosis is visible, as are the overbite, chin in contact with the coffin, and packing material surrounding the neck and behind the head. The punctate bright densities that surround the mummy are real, corresponding to dense inclusions with high mineral content. The mummy's face is longer (from top to bottom) than the icon on the coffin surface. The proportionality of facial components (jaw, midface, orbits, and cranium) are typical of a well-developed, healthy adult. The forehead is flat and the proportion of the face to the cranial cavity are exactly what would be expected in an individual who had no congenital anomalies or developmental defects

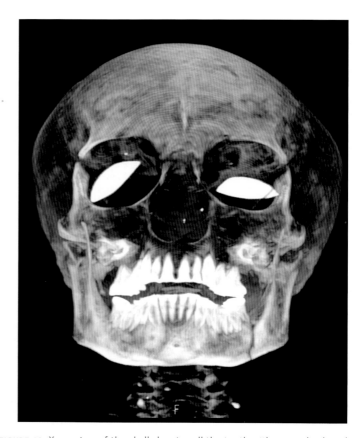

FIGURE 68. X-ray view of the skull showing all the teeth with a non-displaced left jaw fracture (vertical dark line in the mandible). This has no evidence of healing and is presumed to be a post-mortem injury. Notice that the nasal cavity is somewhat featureless, due in part to the procedure where brain contents are removed by inserting a metal probe through the nostril to drain the cranial cavity. Merasamun's right nostril was used for this purpose

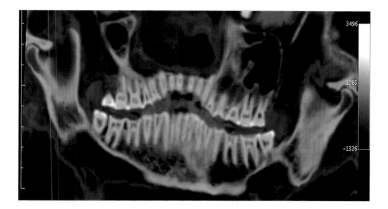

FIGURE 69. Panoramic image of the teeth. This is actually a curved slab through the dental tissues, but has an appearance similar to an orthoptantograph or panorex image obtained frequently today in dental offices as a survey of the teeth and oral bony structures. The upper central incisors are attenuated in this view. All thirty-two teeth are present; the ones shown best are in the mandible (bottom row). There are several key features: no dental decay (caries), wisdom teeth are present and have some signs of wear (only seen in adults), and the dental wear at the tooth crowns is disproportionately high, indicating that Meresamun's diet was unrefined. The periodontal disease that is responsible for most modern human tooth loss is absent, and bone mineralization is substantial. Dental x-rays and especially panoramic views like this one are commonly used in identification of human remains by experts in forensic dentistry

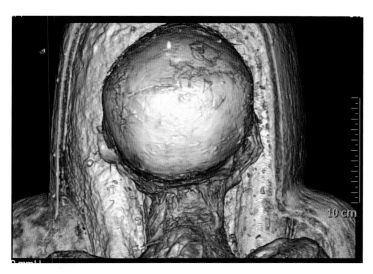

FIGURE 70. The rear of the coffin has been electronically removed, revealing the vertex of the skull. Small, low-set ears are visible bilaterally. The neck has a narrow diameter, consistent with the embalming procedure that removed body fat and moisture. Wrappings are present bilaterally, preventing the head and body from moving within the coffin. Notice that the cranium is symmetric and "normocephalic" with proportions equal to those of modern humans

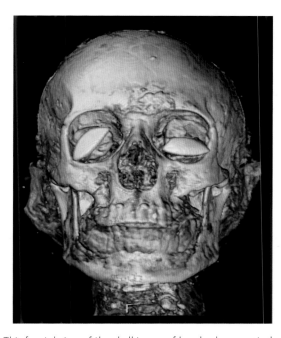

FIGURE 71. This frontal view of the skull is one of hundreds generated with various computer-graphics editing and rendering methods to depict various features of cranial and facial morphology, while discovering the unique characteristics of this individual. This view shows that the lower row of teeth are covered by more than skin, presumably resin. The mouth is slightly agape and the teeth, though all are present without intrinsic decay or bone loss, are not in occlusion due to the overbite. The orbits (eye sockets) have decorative materials (crescent-shaped objects). The eyeballs (ocular globes) are present, but small due to desiccation

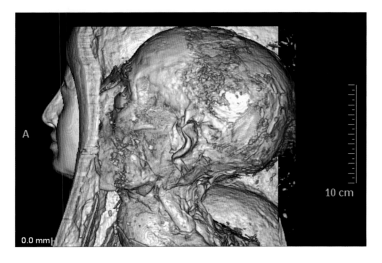

FIGURE 72. The lateral and posterior aspects of the coffin have been electronically removed, revealing the exaggerated angulation and anterior protrusion of the neck (known as cervical lordosis) with the chin touching the coffin anteriorly. This posture was developed in the embalming process and would be unnatural in vivo. The external ear is clearly seen with wrapping material adherent to the skin surface. The skin is intact over the skull. The neck looks thickened anteriorly, due to post-mortem insertion of a large amorphous mass of featureless material, presumably resin. Just above the nose is a remnant of a thick shroud, presumably a moisture barrier

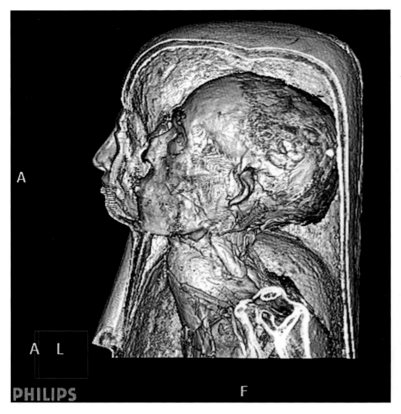

FIGURE 73. Mummy in coffin with left half of the coffin electronically removed. The skin surface can be seen. The neck and torso are shrouded within a presumed moisture barrier. Wrappings are provided in numerous layers

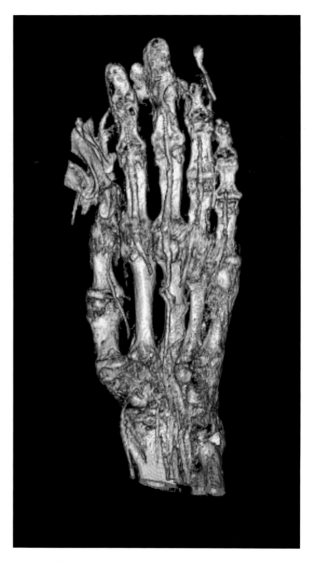

FIGURE 74. Right hand, dorsal view. The wrappings and skin have been partially electronically removed to show the bones of the hand and wrist. All digits are aligned normally with no significant arthritic changes. The extensor tendons for each digit appear as strings that run longitudinally along the surface and extend into the forearm where they attach to individual muscles

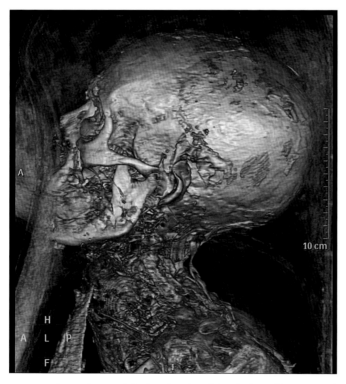

FIGURE 75. Lateral view of the head and neck. With the coffin rendered transparent, the complex wrappings surrounding the neck, the coating of the lower teeth with presumed resin, and the shroud or vapor-barrier extending inferiorly from the middle of the neck are visible

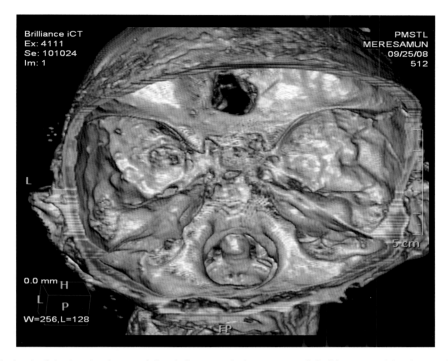

FIGURE 76. Looking from the back of the head with part of the skull removed, the intracranial skull base is visible. This would be the image one would see at autopsy when the brain was excised. There is a midline oval structure at the bottom of the skull base called the foramen magnum, where the spinal cord exits the cranium and attaches to the brainstem. The interior of the cranial cavity retains the membranes that covered the brain itself (often missing in other mummies). The dark hole at the top center of the image is in the frontal region midline where the sense of smell would be present in life. This structure was removed by inserting a probe in the right nostril and puncturing the bony structure (cribiform plate) to remove the brain after death

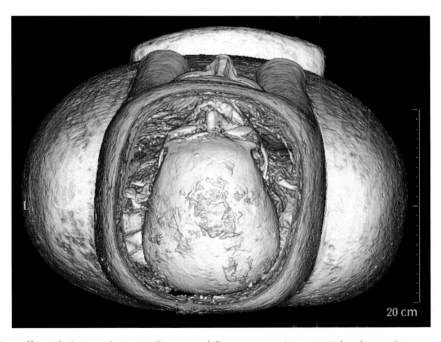

FIGURE 77. Vertex view of the coffin with the top electronically removed. Some preservation material and wrappings are present at the top and surrounding the skull. The coffin icon face and nose can be seen, relative to Merasamun's nose. At the top of the image, the bright horizontal region is due to the feet of the coffin. Most impressive in this image is the asymmetry and misalignment of the various components. The mummy's nose and that of the icon are misaligned. The dense objects in the orbits can be seen bilaterally. The chin is rotated forward (extended) and contacts the coffin near the midline. The feet of the coffin are not in precise alignment with the facial icon. Also note that the skull (cranial cavity) is very symmetric, compatible with normal development and adult age

GLOSSARY

akh — "transfigured spirit"; the spirit of the deceased that was believed to dwell in the afterlife

anthropoid — human shaped

apotropaic — protective

architrave — horizontal architectural element above a doorway

cadastral — adjective derived from the noun "cadaster" indicating a land register

cartonnage — a papier-mâché-type substance made of layers of papyrus or linen, glue, and plaster. Often used for Third Intermediate Period coffins

cession document — a document by which one individual cedes (i.e., transfers) to another the ownership of property

Demotic — cursive script used to write the Egyptian language from about 650 B.C. to the fifth century A.D.

djed pillar — vertical column shape with flaring top and bottom and horizontal cross bars through its upper half; thought to represent the stylized backbone of the god Osiris; by extension with myths of Osiris, the hieroglyph for "stability"

docket — a label listing one or more of the following pieces of information: type of document, parties to document, date of document, date document was filed with the appropriate government agency, the name of that agency, the official who handled the registration

electrum — a naturally occurring alloy of gold and silver

God's Wife of Amun — highest ranking priestess of the Theban god Amun; at times vested with political as well as religious power and authority

hieratic — cursive script used to write the Egyptian language from the Old Kingdom into the third century A.D.

iḥywt — sistrum players

ka — spirit of an individual represented in human form — the part of the soul that needed food offerings in the afterlife

khener (*ḥnr*) — troupe of professional musicians and dancers

medjay — police force of Nubians

naos — a shrine, often the shrine that stood in the sanctuary of a temple and held the statue of the deity who resided in the temple

nbt pr — "mistress of the house" or "owner of the house"

ostracon (pl. ostraca) — flake of stone or a piece of pottery used as a writing surface

sekhem (*sḫm*) — loop-topped sistrum

sesheshet (*sššt*) — naos-form sistrum

shemayet (*šmʿyt*) — ancient Egyptian term for "singer"; *shemayet* could be of various ranks and associated with different deities

situla (pl. situlae) — a handled vessel used in temple and funerary ceremonies; situlae usually contained cool water or milk

stela (pl. stelae) — usually freestanding surface of stone or wood, carved or painted with images and or texts

theophoric — derived from, or incorporating, the name of a god, especially referring to personal names compounded with a divine name

votive — an object that is offered as a part of a vow to a deity; a non-functional replica of an object, usually intended to be offered to a deity or deposited in a tomb

wedjat — stylized representation of an eye and markings of a falcon and a human eyebrow; the *wedjat* is associated with both Horus and Re; the hieroglyphs for "to become whole" and, by extension, "health" and "regeneration"

BIBLIOGRAPHY

Allam, Schafik. *Hieratische Ostraka und Papyri aus der Ramessidenzeit*. Tübingen: Selbstverlag, 1973.

Allen, James P. *The Art of Medicine in Ancient Egypt*. New York: Metropolitan Museum of Art, 2005.

Allen, Thomas George. *Handbook of the Egyptian Collection*. Chicago: University of Chicago Press, 1923.

Altenmüller, H. "Ein Zaubermesser des Mittleren Reiches." *Studien zur altägyptischen Kultur* 13 (1986): 15–16.

Anderson, R. D. *Catalogue of Egyptian Antiquities in the British Museum*, Volume 3: *Musical Instruments*. London: British Museum, 1976.

Andreu, Guillemette; Marie-Hélène Rutschowscaya; and Christiane Ziegler. *Ancient Egypt at the Louvre*. Paris: Hachette, 1997.

Andrews, Carol. *Amulets of Ancient Egypt*. London: British Museum, 1994.

———. *Ancient Egyptian Jewelry*. New York: Harry Abrams, 1990.

Armitage, P. L., and J. Clutton-Brock. "A Radiological and Histological Investigation into the Mummification of Cats from Ancient Egypt." *Journal of Archaeological Science* 8 (1981): 185–96.

Arnold, Dieter. *Temples of the Last Pharaohs*. Oxford: Oxford University Press, 1999.

Aston, Barbara. *Ancient Egyptian Stone Vessels: Materials and Forms*. Studien zur Archäologie und Geschichte Altägyptens 5. Heidelberg: Heidelberger Orientverlag, 1994.

Aston, David. *Egyptian Pottery of the Late New Kingdom and the Third Intermediate Period (Twelfth–Seventh Centuries BC): Tentative Footsteps in Forbidding Terrain*. Studien zur Archäologie und Geschichte Altägyptens 13. Heidelberg: Heidelberger Orientverlag, 1996.

Badawy, Alexander. *A History of Egyptian Architecture: The Empire (the New Kingdom)*. Berkeley and Los Angeles: University of California Press, 1968.

Barber, Elizabeth. *Women's Work: The First 20,000 Years; Women, Cloth and Society in Early Times*. New York: W. W. Norton & Co., 1994.

Blackman, Aylward. "The Position of Women in the Ancient Egyptian Hierarchy." *Journal of Egyptian Archaeology* 7 (1921): 8–20. (Reprinted in *Gods, Priests and Men: Studies in the Religion of Pharaonic Egypt*.... London and New York: Kegan Paul, 1998).

Blyth, Elizabeth. *Karnak: Evolution of a Temple*. London and New York: Routledge, 2006.

Bonnet, Hans. *Reallexikon der ägyptischen Religionsgeschichte*. Berlin and New York: Walter de Gruyter, 1952.

von Bothmer, Bernard. *Antiquities from the Collection of Christos G. Bastis*. Mainz: Philipp von Zabern, 1988.

———. "The Nodding Falcon of the Guennol Collection at the Brooklyn Museum." *Brooklyn Museum Annual* 9 (1967–1968): 75–76.

Breasted, James Henry, Jr. *Egyptian Servant Statues*. Bollingen Series 13. New York: Pantheon, 1948.

Brewer, Douglas, and Emily Teeter. *Egypt and the Egyptians*. 2nd edition. Cambridge: Cambridge University Press, 2007.

Brovarski, Edward; Susan Doll; and Rita Freed (editors). *Egypt's Golden Age: The Art of Living in the New Kingdom, 1558–1085 BC*. Boston: Museum of Fine Arts, 1982.

Brunner-Traut, Emma. "Gravidenflasche: Das Salben des Mutterleibes." In *Archäologie und Altes Testament: Festschrift für Kurt Galling*, edited by Arnulf Kuschke and Ernst Kutsch, pp. 46–47. Tübingen: J. C. B. Mohr, 1970.

Bryan, Betsy. "Evidence for Female Literacy from Theban Tombs of the New Kingdom." *Bulletin of the Egyptological Seminar* 6 (1984): 17–32.

de Buck, A. "The Judicial Papyrus of Turin." *Journal of Egyptian Archaeology* 23 (1937): 152–64.

Capell, Anne, and Glenn Markoe (editors). *Mistress of the House, Mistress of Heaven: Women in Ancient Egypt*. New York: Hudson Hills, 1996.

de Cenival, Françoise. "Un acte de renonciation consécutif à un partage de revenus liturgiques memphites (P. Louvre E 3266)." *Bulletin de l'Institut Français d'Archéologie Orientale, Cairo* 71 (1971): 11–65.

Černý, Jaroslav. "Papyrus Salt 124 (Brit. Mus. 10055)." *Journal of Egyptian Archaeology* 15 (1929): 243–58.

———. "Troisième série de questions adressées aux oracles." *Bulletin de l'Institut Français d'Archéologie Orientale, Cairo* 72 (1972): 49–69.

———. "The Will of Naunakhte and the Related Documents." *Journal of Egyptian Archaeology* 31 (1945): 29–53.

Clère, Pierre. *La Porte d'Évergète à Karnak*. Mémoires publiés par les Membres de l'Institut Français d'Archéologie Orientale du Caire 84. Cairo: Institut Français d'Archéologie Orientale, 1961.

Davies, Norman de Garis. *The Tomb of Antefoker, Vizier of Sesostris I. and of His Wife, Senet (No. 60)*. Theban Tomb Series 2. London: Allen & Unwin, 1920.

———. *The Tomb of Rekh-Mi-Rē' at Thebes*. Metropolitan Museum of Art Egyptian Expedition 11. New York: Metropolitan Museum of Art, 1944.

Davies, Norman de Garis, and R. O. Faulkner. "A Syrian Trading Venture to Egypt." *Journal of Egyptian Archaeology* 33 (1947): 40–46.

Demarée, Robert J. *The ʒḥ iḳr n Rʿ-Stelae: On Ancestor Worship in Ancient Egypt*. Leiden: Nederlands Instituut voor het Nabije Oosten, 1983.

Desroches-Noblecourt, Christiane. *Le Petit Temple d'Abou Simbel*. 2 volumes. Cairo: Centre de Documentation et d'Étude sur l'Ancienne Égypte, 1983.

Doll, S. K. "Bottle in the Form of a Pregnant Woman." In *Egypt's Golden Age: The Art of Living in the New Kingdom, 1558–1085 B.C.*, edited by Edward Brovarski et al., p. 293. Boston: Museum of Fine Arts, 1982.

Edwards, I. E. S. *Oracular Amuletic Decrees of the Late New Kingdom*. Hieratic Papyri in the British Museum, fourth series. London: Trustees of the British Museum, 1960.

Epigraphic Survey. *Medinet Habu*, Volume 5: *The Temple Proper, Part 1: The Portico, the Treasury, and Chapels Adjoining the First Hypostyle Hall, with Marginal Material from the Forecourts*. Oriental Institute Publications 83. Chicago: University of Chicago Press, 1957.

———. *Reliefs and Inscriptions from Luxor Temple*, Volume 1: *The Festival Procession of Opet in the Colonnade Hall*. Oriental Institute Publications 107. Chicago: Oriental Institute, 1994.

———. *Reliefs and Inscriptions at Karnak*, Volume 1: *Ramses III's Temple within the Great Inclosure of Amon, Part 1*. Oriental Institute Publications 25. Chicago: University of Chicago Press, 1936.

———. *Reliefs and Inscriptions at Karnak*, Volume 2: *Ramses III's Temple within the Great Inclosure of Amon, Part 2; and Ramses III's Temple in the Precinct of Mut*. Oriental Institute Publications 35. Chicago: University of Chicago, 1936.

———. *Reliefs and Inscriptions at Karnak*, Volume 3: *Bubastite Portal*. Oriental Institute Publications 74. Chicago: University of Chicago Press, 1954.

———. *The Temple of Khonsu*, Volume 1: *Scenes of King Herihor in the Court*. Oriental Institute Publications 100. Chicago: Oriental Institute, 1979.

———. *The Temple of Khonsu*, Volume 2: *Scenes and Inscriptions in the Court and the First Hypostyle Hall*. Oriental Institute Publications 103. Chicago: Oriental Institute, 1981.

———. *The Tomb of Kheruef: Theban Tomb 192*. Oriental Institute Publications 102. Chicago: Oriental Institute, 1980.

Faulkner, R. O. "The Admonitions of an Egyptian Sage." *Journal of Egyptian Archaeology* 51 (1965): 53–62.

Fazzini, Richard. *Egypt: Dynasty XXII–XXV*. Iconography of Religions 16, fascicle 10. Leiden: E. J. Brill, 1988.

Fischer, Henry George. *Egyptian Women of the Old Kingdom and of the Heracleopolitan Period*. 2nd edition. New York: Metropolitan Museum of Art, 2000.

Foster, John. *Echoes of Egyptian Voices*. Norman: University of Oklahoma, 1992.

Frankfurter, David. *Religion in Roman Egypt: Assimilation and Resistance*. Princeton: Princeton University Press, 1998.

Gardiner, A. H. "Adoption Extraordinary." *Journal of Egyptian Archaeology* 26 (1940): 23–29.

———. "A Lawsuit Arising from the Purchase of Two Slaves." *Journal of Egyptian Archaeology* 21 (1935): 140–46.

———. "The Dakhleh Stela." *Journal of Egyptian Archaeology* 19 (1933): 19–30.

———. *The Inscriptions of Mes: A Contribution to the Study of Egyptian Judicial Procedure*. Untersuchungen zur Geschichte und Altertumskunde Ägyptens 4/3. Leipzig: Hinrichs, 1905.

———. *The Wilbour Papyrus* Oxford: Oxford University Press, 1948.

Green, Christine Insley. *The Temple Furniture from the Sacred Animal Necropolis at North Saqqâra 1964–1976*. Excavation Memoir London 53: Egypt Exploration Society, 1987.

Habachi, Labib. "The Clearance of the Tomb of Kheruef at Thebes (1957–1958)." *Annales du Service des Antiquités de Égypt* 55 (1958): 326–60.

Helck, Wolfgang. *Die datieren und datierbaren Ostraka, Papyri und Graffiti von Deir el-Medineh*. Ägyptologische Abhandlungen 63. Wiesbaden: Harrassowitz, 2002.

———. *Die Ritualszenen auf der Umfassungsmauer Ramses' II. in Karnak*. Ägyptologische Abhandlungen 18. Wiesbaden: Harrassowitz, 1968.

Hickman, Hans. "La Menat." *Kemi* 13 (1954): 99–102.

———. "Le Métier de Musicien." *Cahiers d'Histoire Égyptienne* 6 (December 1954): 299–314.

Hill, Marsha (editor). *Gifts for the Gods: Image from Egyptian Temples*. New York: Metropolitan Museum of Art, 2007.

Hölscher, Uvo. *The Excavation of Medinet Habu*, Volume 2: *The Temples of the Eighteenth Dynasty*. Oriental Institute Publications 41. Chicago: University of Chicago Press, 1939.

——. *The Excavation of Medinet Habu*, Volume 4: *The Mortuary Temple of Ramses III*. Oriental Institute Publications 55. Chicago: University of Chicago Press, 1951.

——. *The Excavation of Medinet Habu*, Volume 5: *Post Ramessid Remains*. Oriental Institute Publications 56. Chicago: University of Chicago Press, 1954.

Hughes, George R., and Richard Jasnow. *Oriental Institute Hawara Papyri, Demotic and Greek Texts from an Egyptian Family Archive in the Fayum (Fourth to Third Century B.C.)*. Oriental Institute Publications 113. Chicago: Oriental Institute, 1997.

Ikram, Salima, and Aidan Dodson. *The Mummy in Ancient Egypt: Equipping the Dead for Eternity*. London: Thames & Hudson, 1998.

Jacquet-Gordon, Helen. *The Temple of Khonsu*, Volume 3: *The Graffiti on the Khonsu Temple Roof at Karnak: A Manifestation of Personal Piety*. Oriental Institute Publications 123. Chicago: Oriental Institute, 2003.

Janssen, Jac. "Marriage Problems and Public Reactions." In *Pyramid Studies and Other Essays Presented to I. E. S. Edwards*, edited by John Baines, pp, 134–37. Occasional Publications 7. London: Egypt Exploration Society, 1988.

Johnson, Janet H. "'Annuity Contracts' and Marriage." In *For His Ka, Essays Offered in Memory of Klaus Baer*, edited by David P. Silverman, pp. 113–32. Studies in Ancient Oriental Civilization 55. Chicago: Oriental Institute, 1994.

——. "Speculations on Middle Kingdom Marriage." In *Studies on Ancient Egypt in Honour of H. S. Smith*, edited by Anthony Leahy and W. J. Tait, pp. 169–72. Occasional Publications 13. London: Egypt Exploration Society, 1999.

——. "Women, Wealth and Work in Egyptian Society of the Ptolemaic Period." In *Egyptian Religion, The Last Thousand Years: Studies Dedicated to the Memory of Jan Quaegebeur*, edited by W. Clarysse, A. Schoors, and H. Willems, pp. 1393–1421. Orientalia Lovaniensia Analecta 85. Leuven: Peeters, 1998.

Jones, Dilwyn. *An Index of Ancient Egyptian Titles, Epithets and Phrases of the Old Kingdom*. British Archaeological Reports, International Series 866. Oxford: Archaeopress, 2000.

Katary, Sally L. D. *Land Tenure in the Ramesside Period*. Studies in Egyptology. London: Kegan Paul International, 1989.

Kemp, Barry. *Ancient Egypt: Anatomy of a Civilization*. London and New York, Routledge, 1989.

Kitchen, Kenneth A. *Ramesside Inscriptions: Historical and Biographical*, Volume 7. Oxford: B. H. Blackwell, 1989.

——. *The Third Intermediate Period in Egypt (1100–650 B.C.)*. Warminster: Aris & Phillips, 1986.

Leclant, Jean. "Sur un contrepoids de menat au nom de Taharqa." *Mèlanges Mariette*. Bibliothèque d'Études 32, pp. 251–84. Cairo: Institut Français d'Archéologie Orientale, 1961.

Legrain, Georges Albert. *Cairo Catalogue General*, Volume 3: *Statues et statuettes de rois et des particuliers*. Cairo: L'Institut Français d'Archéologie Orientale, 1914.

van Lieven, Alexandra. "Musical Notation in Roman Period Egypt." *Studien zur Musikarchäologie* 3, edited by Ellen Hickmann, Anne D. Kilmer, and Ricardo Eichmann, pp. 497–510. Orient-Archäologie 10. Rahden/Westf.: Marie Leidorf, 2002.

Le Poole, H. A. C. "Behen Oil: A Classic Oil for Modern Cosmetics." *Cosmetics and Toiletries* 111 (1996): 77–80.

Lichtheim, Miriam. *Ancient Egyptian Literature: A Book of Readings*, Volume 2: *The New Kingdom*. Berkeley: University of California Press, 1976.

——. "Situla No. 11395 and Some Remarks on Egyptian Situlae." *Journal of Near Eastern Studies* 6 (1947): 169–79.

Logan, T. "The *Jmyt-pr* Document: Form, Function, and Significance." *Journal of the American Research Center in Egypt* 37 (2000): 49–74.

Lüddeckens, Erich. *Ägyptische Eheverträge*. Wiesbaden: Harrassowitz, 1960.

Lüddeckens, Erich; Rolf Wassermann; W. Erichsen; and Charles Francis Nims. *Demotische Urkunden aus Hawara*. Verzeichnis der orientalischen Handschriften in Deutschland, Supplementband 28. Stuttgart: Franz Steiner, 1998.

Manning, J. G. "Land and Status in Ptolemaic Egypt: The Status Designation 'Occupation Title + B ̣k + Divine Name.'" In *Grund und Boden in Altägypten (Rechtliche und sozio-ökonomische Verhältnisse): Akten des internationalen Symposions, Tübingen 18.–20. Juni 1990*, edited by Schafik Allam, pp. 147–75. Tübingen: n.p., 1994.

Mattha, G., and George R. Hughes. *The Demotic Legal Code of Hermopolis West*. Bibliothèque d'Étude 45. Cairo: l'Institut Français d'Archéologie Orientale, 1975.

McDowell, Andrea G. *Jurisdiction in the Workmen's Community at Deir el-Medina*. Egyptologische uitgaven 5. Leiden: Nederlands Instituut voor het Nabije Oosten, 1990.

Malek, Jaromir. *The Cat in Ancient Egypt*. London: British Museum, 1993.

Manniche, Lise. *Lost Tombs: A Study of Certain Eighteenth Dynasty Monuments in the Theban Necropolis*. London: Kegan Paul International, 1988.

———. *Music and Musicians in Ancient Egypt*. London: British Museum, 1991.

Marfoe, Leon. *A Guide to the Oriental Institute Museum*. Chicago: Oriental Institute, 1982.

Martin, Geoffrey T. *The Hidden Tombs of Memphis*. New York: Thames & Hudson, 1991.

———. *The Tomb of Hetepka and Other Reliefs and Inscriptions from the Sacred Animal Necropolis, North Saqqâra, 1964–1973*. Texts from Excavations, Memoir 4. London: Egypt Exploration Society, 1979.

Morris, Ellen. "Vase in the Shape of a Lutenist." In *Searching for Ancient Egypt: Art, Architecture, and Artifacts from the University of Pennsylvania Museum of Archaeology and Anthropology*, edited by David P. Silverman, p. 237. Dallas: Dallas Museum of Art/University of Pennsylvania Museum, 1997.

Murnane, William. *Texts from the Amarna Period in Egypt*. Atlanta: Scholars Press, 1995.

Munro, Peter. *Die spätägyptischen Totenstelen*. Ägyptische Forschungen 25. Glückstadt: J. J. Augustin, 1973.

Murray, Mary Anne. "Brewing and Baking." In *Ancient Egyptian Materials and Technology*, edited by Paul Nicholson and Ian Shaw, pp. 537–76. Cambridge: Cambridge University Press, 2000.

Mysiliwiec, Karol. *The Twilight of Ancient Egypt*. Ithaca: Cornell University Press, 2000.

Naguib, Saphinaz-Amal. *Le clergé féminine d'Amon thébain*. Orientalia Lovaniensia Analecta 38. Louvain: Peeters, 1990.

Nagy, István. *Guide to the Egyptian Collection*. Budapest: Museum of Fine Arts, 1999.

Naville, Edouard. *The Festival Hall of Osorkon*. Memoir of the Egypt Exploration Fund 10. London: Kegan Paul, Trench, Trübner & Co., 1892.

Nord, Del. "The Term ḥnr: 'Harem' of Musical Performers'?" In *Studies in Ancient Egypt, the Aegean, and the Sudan: Essays in Honor of Dows Dunham on the Occasion of His 90th Birthday, June 1, 1980*, edited by William. K. Simpson and W. M. Davis, pp. 137–45. Boston: Museum of Fine Arts, 1981.

Nims, C. F. "A Demotic 'Document of Endowment' from the Time of Nectanebo I." *Mitteilungen des Deutschen Archäologischen Instituts, Abteilung Kairo* 16 (1958): 237–46.

Onstine, Suzanne. *The Role of the Chantress (Šmʿyt) in Ancient Egypt*. British Archaeological Reports, International Series 1401. Oxford: Archaeopress, 2005.

Otto, E. *Die biographischen Inschriften der ägyptischen Spatzeit, Ihre Geistesgeschichtliche und Literarische Bedeutung*. Leiden: Brill, 1954.

Peet, T. Eric. *The Great Tomb-Robberies of the Twentieth Egyptian Dynasty*. Oxford: Clarendon Press, 1930.

Pestman, P. W. *Les Papyrus démotiques de Tsenhor (P. Tsenhor): Les archives privées d'une femme égyptienne du temps de Darius Iᵉʳ*. Studia Demotica 4. Leuven: Peeters, 1994.

———. "Appearance and Reality in Written Contracts: Evidence from Bilingual Family Archives." In *Legal Documents of the Hellenistic World: Papers from a Seminar Arranged by the Institute of Classical Studies, the Institute of Jewish Studies and the Warburg Institute, University of London, February to May 1986*, edited by M. J. Geller and Herwig Maehler, pp. 79–87. London: Warburg Institute, University of London, 1995.

Petrie, W. M. Flinders, and A. C. Mace. *Diospolis Parva: The Cemeteries of Abadiyeh and Hu, 1889–99*. Excavation Memoirs 20. London: Egypt Exploration Society, 1901 (reprinted 1977).

Pinch, Geraldine. *Magic in Ancient Egypt*. London: British Museum, 1994.

Porter, Bertha, and Rosalind L. B. Moss. *Topographical Bibliography of Ancient Egyptian Hieroglyphic Texts, Reliefs, and Paintings*, Volume 1: *The Theban Necropolis*, Part 1: *Private Tombs*. 2nd edition. Oxford: Griffith Institute, 1960.

Quibell, James. *The Ramesseum*. Egypt Exploration Fund Memoir 2. London: The Egyptian Exploration Fund, 1896.

Raven, M. J. (editor). *Pharaonic and Early Medieval Egyptian Textiles*. Collections of the National Museum of Antiquities at Leiden 8. Leiden: Rijksmuseum van Oudheden, 1994

Ray, John D. "The Archive of Ḥor." *Texts from Excavations, Second Memoir*. London: Egypt Exploration Society, 1975.

Redford, Donald; Sara Orel; Susan Redford; and Steven Shubert. "East Karnak Excavations, 1987–1989." *Journal of the American Research Center in Egypt* 28 (1991): 75–106.

Riefstahl, Elizabeth. *Patterned Textiles in Pharaonic Egypt*. Brooklyn: Brooklyn Museum, 1944.

Ritner, Robert. "Denderite Temple Hierarchy and the Family of the Theban High Priest Nebwenenef: Block Statue OIM 10729." In *For His Ka: Essays Offered in Memory of Klaus Baer*, edited by David P. Silverman, pp. 205–26. Studies in Ancient Oriental Civilization 55. Chicago: Oriental Institute, 1994.

———. "Fictive Adoptions or Celibate Princesses?" *Göttinger Miszellen* 164 (1998): 85–90.

———. *The Libyan Anarchy: Documents from Egypt's Third Intermediate Period*. Writings from the Ancient World. Atlanta: Society of Biblical Literature, In press.

———. "Magical Wand." *Searching for Ancient Egypt: Art, Architecture, and Artifacts from the University of Pennsylvania Museum of Archaeology and Anthropology*, edited by David P. Silverman, pp. 234–35. Dallas: Dallas Museum of Art/University of Pennsylvania Museum, 1997.

———. "Third Intermediate Period Antecedents of Demotic Legal Terminology." In *Acts of the Seventh International Conference of Demotic Studies: Copenhagen, 23–27 August 1999*, edited by Kim Ryholt, pp. 343–59. CNI Publications 27. Copenhagen: Carsten Niebuhr Institute of Near Eastern Studies, University of Copenhagen, 2002.

———. "An Oblique Reference to the Expelled High Priest Osorkon?" In *Gold of Praise: Studies on Ancient Egypt in Honor of Edward F. Wente*, edited by Emily Teeter and John Larson, pp. 351–60. Studies in Ancient Oriental Civilization 58. Chicago: Oriental Institute, 1999.

Robins, Gay. "Some Principles of Compositional Dominance and Gender Hierarchy in Egyptian Art," *Journal of the American Research Center in Egypt* 31 (1994): 33–40.

———. "Women and Children in Peril: Pregnancy, Birth, and Infant Mortality in Ancient Egypt." *KMT* 5: 1994/1995: 24–35.

———. *Women in Ancient Egypt*. Cambridge: Harvard University, 1993.

Roeder, Günther. *Ägyptische Bronzefiguren*. Mitteilungen aus der Ägyptischen Sammlung 6. Berlin: Staatliche Museen zu Berlin, 1956.

Roehrig, Catharine. "Woman's Work: Some Occupations of Non-royal Women as Depicted in Ancient Egyptian Art." In *Mistress of the House, Mistress of Heaven: Women in Ancient Egypt*, edited by Anne K. Capel and Glenn E. Markoe, pp. 13–24. New York: Hudson Hills, 1996.

Romano, James F. "Jar in the Form of a Woman." In *Mistress of the House, Mistress of Heaven: Women in Ancient Egypt*, edited by Anne K. Capel and Glenn E. Markoe, p. 63. New York: Hudson Hills, 1996.

Roth, Ann Macy. "Father Earth, Mother Sky." In *Reading the Body, Representations and Remains in the Archaeological Record*, edited by Alison E. Rautman, pp. 187–201. Regendering the Past. Philadelphia: University of Pennsylvania, 2000.

———. "Gender Roles in Ancient Egypt." In *A Companion to the Ancient Near East*, edited by Daniel C. Snell, pp. 211–18. Oxford: Blackwell, 2005.

———. "Little Women: Gender and Hierarchic Proportion in Old Kingdom Mastaba Chapels." In *The Old Kingdom Art and Archaeology: Proceedings of the Conference Held in Prague, May 31–June 4, 2004*, edited by Miroslav Bárta, pp. 281–96 Prague: Czech Institute of Egyptology, 2006.

———. "The Meaning of Menial Labor: 'Servant Statues' in Old Kingdom Serdabs." *Journal of the American Research Center in Egypt* 39 (2002): 103–21.

Rowlandson, Jane (editor). *Women and Society in Greek and Roman Egypt: A Sourcebook*. Cambridge: Cambridge University Press, 1998.

Samuel, Delwen. "Brewing and Baking." In *Ancient Egyptian Materials and Technology*, edited by Paul Nicholson and Ian Shaw, pp. 537–76. Cambridge: Cambridge University Press, 2000.

Schott, Siegfried. *Das schöne Fest von Wüstentale: Festbraüche einer Totenstadt*. Abhandlungen der geistes- und sozialwissenschaftlichen Klasse Mainz 11. Mainz: Akademie der Wissenschaften und der Literatur in Mainz, 1953.

Sherman, Elizabeth. "Djedḥor the Saviour Statue Base, OI 10589." *Journal of Egyptian Archaeology* 67 (1981): 82–102, pls. 13–14.

Shorter, Alan. "The Tomb of Aaḥmose, Supervisor of the Mysteries of the House of the Morning." *Journal of Egyptian Archaeology* 16 (1930): 54–62.

Simpson, William K. (editor). *The Literature of Ancient Egypt*. Yale University Press: New Haven and London, 2003.

Strouhal, Eugen. "Queen Mutnodjmet at Memphis: Anthropological and Paleopathological Evidence." In *L'égyptologie in 1979*, vol. 2, edited by Jean Leclant, pp. 317–22. Paris: Éditions du Centre National de la Recherche Scientifique, 1982.

Taylor, John. *Mummy: The Inside Story*. London: British Museum, 2004.

———. "The Third Intermediate Period." In *The Oxford History of Egypt*, edited by Ian Shaw, pp. 330–68. Oxford: Oxford University Press, 2000.

Teeter, Emily. *Ancient Egypt: Treasures from the Collection of the Oriental Institute University of Chicago*. Oriental Institute Museum Publications 23. Chicago: Oriental Institute, 2003.

———. "Animal Figurines." In *The American Discovery of Ancient Egypt*, edited by Nancy Thomas, p. 195. Los Angeles: Los Angeles County Museum of Art, 1995.

———. *Baked Clay Figurines and Votive Beds from Medinet Habu*. Oriental Institute Publications 133. Chicago: Oriental Institute, 2008.

———. "Diesehebsed, a ḥst ḥnw n Imn at Medinet Habu." *Varia Aegyptiaca* 10 (1994): no. 203, pp. 195–203.

———. "Female Musicians in Ancient Egypt." In *Rediscovering the Muses: Women's Musical Traditions*, edited by Kimberly Marshall, pp. 68–91. Boston: Northeastern University Press, 1993.

———. "Piety at Medinet Habu." *Oriental Institute News & Notes* 173 (Spring, 2002), pp. 1–6.

————. *Scarabs, Scaraboids, Seals, and Seal Impressions from Medinet Habu.* Oriental Institute Publications 118. Chicago: Oriental Institute, 2003.

Thompson, Dorothy. *Egypt Under the Ptolemies.* Princeton: Princeton University Press, 1988.

Thompson, Herbert. *A Family Archive from Siut, from Papyri in the British Museum.* Oxford: Oxford University Press, 1934.

Toivari-Viitala, Jaana. *Women at Deir el-Medina.* Leiden: Nederlands Instituut voor het Nabije Oosten, 2001.

Troy, Lana. *Patterns of Queenship in Ancient Egyptian Myth and History.* Acta Universitatis Upsaliensis Boreas 14. Stockholm: Almquist & Wiksell, 1986.

van Rooij, E. H. C., and G. M. Vogelsang-Eastwood. "The Pharaonic Textiles." In *Pharaonic and Early Medieval Egyptian Textiles,* edited by M. J. Raven, pp. 11–136. Leiden: Rijksmuseum van Oudheden, 1994.

Vandier, Jacques. *Manuel d'archéologie égyptienne,* Volume 4, *Bas-reliefs et peintures: Scènes de la vie quotidienne.* Paris: A. & J. Picard, 1964.

Vernus, Pascal. *Athribis: Textes et documents relatifs à la géographie, aux cultes, et à l'histoire d'une ville du delta égyptien à l'époque pharaonique.* Bibliothèque d' Étude 74. Cairo: Institut Français d'Archéologie Orientale du Caire, 1978.

Vittmann, G. *Der demotische Papyrus Rylands 9.* Ägypten und Altes Testament 38. Wiesbaden: Harrassowitz, 1998.

Vogelsang-Eastwood, Gillan. *Pharaonic Egyptian Clothing.* Leiden: E. J. Brill, 1993.

————. *The Production of Linen in Pharaonic Egypt.* Leiden: Textile Research Center, 1992.

————. "Textiles." In *Ancient Egyptian Materials and Technology,* edited by Paul Nicholson and Ian Shaw, pp. 268–98. Cambridge: Cambridge University Press, 2000.

Wente, Edward F. *Letters from Ancient Egypt.* Atlanta: Scholars Press, 1990.

Williams, Bruce. *Meroitic Remains from Qustul Cemetery Q, Ballana Cemetery B, and a Ballana Settlement.* 2 volumes. Oriental Institute Nubian Expedition 8. Chicago: Oriental Institute, 1991.

Wilson, Karen, and Joan Barghusen. *Highlights from the Collection.* Chicago: Oriental Institute, 1989.

Young, Eric. "A Possible Consanguineous Marriage in the Time of Philip Arrhidaeus." *Journal of the American Research Center in Egypt* 4 (1965): 69–71.

Yoyotte, Jean. "The Divine Adoratrices of Amun." In *Queens of Egypt: From Hatshepsut to Cleopatra,* edited by Christiane Ziegler, pp. 174–82. Monaco: Grimaldi Forum, 2008.

CHECKLIST OF THE EXHIBIT

MERESAMUN'S EGYPT

10797	Coffin and mummy of Meresamun

INSIDE THE TEMPLE

5518	Clap stick
9458	Figurine of Bastet
10589	Family of temple musicians
10590	Relief of dancers and singers
10681	Bronze menat
11394	Ritual vessel (situla)
14058	Sistrum
14767	Relief of sistrum player
17570	Menat counterpoise
19474	Harp
1351	Offering to the God
10578	Ritual vase
12296	Record of delivery of provisions from temple
10504	Oracle statue
18876	Oracular inquiry
701	Mummified crocodile
9237	Mummified ibis
11390	Bronze cat statuette
25605	Coffin for lizard

MERESAMUN'S LIFE OUTSIDE THE TEMPLE

Home Furnishings

7182	Bottle in the shape of a hedgehog
26140	Bowl
26141	Open bowl
29302	Jar

Personal Grooming

5352	Tweezers
7201	Comb
8785	Hair pin
14426	Razor
16874	Mirror
18185	Hair styling tool

Jewelry

5524	Beads
8824a	Beads
8824c	Beads
10427	Tubular beads
13665	Ball and barrel beads
14563	Ear spool
15067	Beads with stone cowrie shells
15082	Disk beads
15313	Hair ring
15314	Hair ring
15315	Hair ring
15562	Ear spool

Cosmetic Vessels

11316	Cosmetic jar
11321	Cosmetic jar
11326	Cosmetic jar
11345	Cosmetic jar
14542	Cosmetic jar

Household Cults

16718	Ear stela
14287	Ancestor cult stela
14768	Votive footprint
14776	Votive bed
14613	Female figurine
14594	Female figurine
14583	Female figurine

Fertility and Birth Rituals

10089	Taweret amulet
10788	Magic knife
11313	Pregnancy ointment jar
14948	Frog amulet
17500	Bes amulet
18286	Pectoral
25622a–d	Oracular amuletic decree

Legal and Social Rights of Women in Egypt

17481	Annuity contract
18280	Stela of a mistress of the house
25263	Transfer of property to a woman

Women and Their Employment

Spinning Equipment

569	Spindle whorl
7113	Spindle whorl
16899	Textile
17112	Spindle whorl
22527c	Spindle
27369	Spinning bowl

Servant Statues

10622	Statue of woman grinding grain
10635	Statue of woman mashing beer

CONCORDANCE OF ORIENTAL INSTITUTE MUSEUM REGISTRATION NUMBERS

OIM Registration Number	Catalog or Figure Number	Description
569	66	Spindle whorl
701	17	Mummified crocodile
1351	11	Stela
5352	29	Tweezers
5518	3	Clap stick
5524	32	Beads
6739	Fig. 41	Stela
7182	24	Bottle in the shape of a hedgehog
7201	25	Comb
8785	28	Hair pin
8824a	31	Beads
8824c	33	Beads
9237	18	Mummified ibis
9238	Fig. 35	Mummified ibis
9458	8	Figurine of Bastet
10089	58	Taweret amulet
10427	35	Tubular beads
10504	15	Oracle statue
10578	13	Ritual vase
10589	2	Family of temple musicians
10590	10	Relief of dancers and singers
10622	71	Statue of woman grinding grain
10635	72	Statue of woman mashing beer
10681	6	Aegis
10718	Fig. 23	Sistrum
10729	Fig. 6	Block statue of Basa
10788	55	Magic knife
10797	1	Coffin and mummy of Meresamun
11189	Fig. 39	Serpent coffin

OIM Registration Number	Catalog or Figure Number	Description
11313	56	Pregnancy ointment jar
11316	46	Cosmetic jar
11321	47	Cosmetic jar
11326	45	Cosmetic jar
11345	43	Cosmetic jar
11394	12	Ritual vessel (situla)
11390	19	Bronze cat statuette
12296	14	Record of delivery of provisions from temple
13665	34	Ball and barrel beads
14058	4	Sistrum
14287	49	Ancestor cult stela
14426	30	Razor
14542	44	Cosmetic jar
14563	38	Ear spool
14583	53	Female figurine
14594	52	Female figurine
14613	54	Female figurine
14681	Fig. 15	Fragment of relief of Diesehebsed with Amunirdis
14767	5	Relief of sistrum player
14768	50	Votive footprint
14776	51	Votive bed
14948	60	Frog amulet
15067	36	Beads with stone cowrie shells
15082	37	Disk beads
15313	40	Hair ring
15314	41	Hair ring
15315	42	Hair ring
15562	39	Ear spool
16718	48	Ear stela
16874	26	Mirror

OIM Registration Number	Catalog or Figure Number	Description
16899	65	Textile
17006	Fig. 51	Sketch
17112	67	Spindle whorl
17113	68	Whorl
17481	62	Annuity contract
17500	59	Bes amulet
17570	7	Menat counterpoise
18185	27	Hair styling tool
18280	64	Stela of a mistress of the house
18286	57	Pectoral
18826	Fig. 38	Cat mask

OIM Registration Number	Catalog or Figure Number	Description
18876	16	Oracular inquiry
19474	9	Harp
22527c	69	Spindle with whorl
25263	63	Transfer of property to a woman
25605	20	Coffin for lizard
25622	61	Oracular amuletic decree
26140	21	Bowl
26141	22	Open bowl
27369	70	Spinning bowl
29302	23	Jar

INDEX OF EGYPTIAN NAMES

ROYAL NAMES

Ahmose Nofertari — fig. 29
Alexander the Great — 13
Amasis — fig. 23
Amunhotep I — 48
Amunhotep II — 44-45
Amunhotep III — 32, 37; figs. 14, 20, 33-34
Amunirdis — fig. 5
Amunirdis II — figs. 4, 15
Amunrud — 29
Arsinoe — 47
Darius I — 84
Hatshepsut — fig. 19
Horemheb — 32, 37, 46, 76, 79
Isis — fig. 51
Maatkare — 90
Meritaten — 35
Mutnedjmet — 76
Neferu — fig. 47
Nimlot — 13, 15
Niuserre — 108-09
Osorkon I — 13, 29
Osorkon II — 13, 28
Osorkon III — 13, 17; fig. 5
Osorkon IV — 13
Osorkon, Prince — 13, 15, 17; fig. 1
Piankhy — see Piye
Piye (Piankhy) — 16
Ptolemy III — 32, 95
Ramesses II (the Great) — 15, 32, 45, 100; fig. 56
Ramesses III — 26; fig. 31
Ramesses VI — fig. 51
Shepenwepet I — 17; fig. 3
Shepenwepet II — fig. 16
Sheshonq I — 13, 16-17, 88-89; fig. 53
Sheshonq II — 13
Sheshonq III — 13, 16
Sheshonq V — 13
Sit-Hathor — 35
Smendes — 13
Taharqa — 17, 82; fig. 2
Takelot I — 13
Takelot II — 13, 15, 29
Theodosius — 49
Thutmose I — 45-46
Thutmose III — 15
Tiy — 35
Tutankhamun — 26-27, 35

PRIVATE NAMES

Ankh-merwer — 92, 95-96
Amenemhet — 29, 31
Ankhaf — 91
Antefoqer — 35; fig. 27
Bakwerel — 72
Basa — 129; fig. 6
Bastet-iyw — 33-34
Diesehebsed — 29, 82, 129; figs. 15-16
Diesenesyt — 97
Djari — fig. 57
Djedhor — 33-34
Djed-Khonsu-iw-ef-Ankh — 73
Djed-Khonsu-iw-es-Ankh — 43
Djehutynefer — fig. 50
Epiphanius — 107
Ḥenutnetjeru — 89
Henuttawy — 90, 103
Her-ankh — 95-96
Herere — 27
Huy — 46, 59
Irer — 99
Iuput — 13
Iuwelot — 13, 90
Kemena — fig. 21
Kenamun — 102; fig. 58
Kheruef — 28, 42; figs. 9, 14, 20, 33-34
Khnumhotep — 99; fig. 55
Khons — fig. 30
Khut — 33
Meresamun — 15-19, 21-28, 30, 35, 43-45, 55, 57-58, 60,
        73, 75-76, 82, 84-85, 87-88, 90, 97-98, 100-03,
        108, 111-12, 127, 129; figs. 9-10, 13, 46
Meresamunet — 29, 60
Merit — 109
Mery — fig. 26
Merymaat — 102
Mes — 88
Minnakht — figs. 40, 43
Montuemhat — 29, 82, 91
Mutenope — 103
Nakht — 72
Nakhtamun — fig. 21
Nakht-Mut — 86-87, 91; fig. 52
Naunakht — 91
Nebamun — 58; figs. 32, 44
Nebet-em-pet — 108-09
Neferrenpet — 100; figs. 49, 56

Nesamenope — 103

Nes-Mut — 88

Nespeqashuty — 97

Nikauinpu — 108–09

Nysu-Bastet — 88–89, 91; fig. 53

Paankhenamun — fig. 7

Padi — 89

Padi-Isis — 85–86

Paseny — 103

Pasur — 46

Pedjodj — 89

Pedubast — 16

Pen-maa — 44

Peset — 44

Rekhmire — 29; figs. 24, 54

Senbu — fig. 41

Seneb — fig. 48

Sennedjem — fig. 42

Sennefer — fig. 26

Ser-Djhuty — 43

Seth-nakht — 91

Sethmose — 72

Shepen-Isis — see Tasherien-Mut

Shepet-en-Khonsu — fig. 9

Tabaket — 48

Ta-baket-en-ese — 44

Tamit — 72

Tasherien-Mut (Shepen-Isis) — 87–88

Ta-sherit-(en)-taihet — 33

Ta-sherit-en-tayisw — 33

Tawy-henewt-Mut — fig. 8

Tayhesi — 33

Tayhor — 33–34

Tay-iru — 96

Tayuhenut — 88–89

Tetisheri — 80–81

Tines-Mut — 88

Tjaynefer — 27

Tsenhor — 84, 88, 90–91

Wayhes — 89, 91; fig. 53

Wenamon — 19

GENERAL INDEX

administration, temple — 15, 17, 103

Admonisions of Ipuwer — 101

adoption — 57, 82, 88, 90

Adoption Papyrus — 90

aegis — 37–38, 129; figs. 29–30

Aha ("the fighter") — 77

akh (spirit), cult of — 72

alabastron (pl. alabastra) — 69

Alexandria — 10, 47

Amun — 15–17; figs. 3–4, 7–8

Amun-Re — 15, 27, 32, 43, 87; figs. 8

ancestor cult — 71

animal cult — 49

ankh — 45, 80

annuity contracts — 86–87, 90, 92–96

Apanage Stela — 84

Apis — 23, 49

Apophis — 49

Assyrians — 13, 16

Athena — 38

Athribis — 12, 31, 49

baking — 57, 101, 109

Ba-neb-djed — 23

Bastet — 36–37, 40, 49, 52

Bat — 25

beads — 39, 62, 66–67

Beni Hasan — 99; fig. 55

Bes — 36, 74, 76–77, 79; fig. 22

block statue — 18–19; fig. 6

Book of the Dead — 18, 44, 98; fig. 8

brewing — 55, 57, 101–02, 109

bronze — 18, 30, 36–40, 47, 49, 52–53, 63–65

bronze working — 18

Bubastis — 40

Bubastieion — 52

Bubastite Court — 17; fig. 2

Bubastite Portal — 15; fig. 1

cartonnage — 18, 21–23; figs. 7, 9

cat — 36, 40, 52; figs. 36, 38

catacomb (ibis) — 49; fig. 37

celibacy — 24

cession document — 95–96

Chapel of Osiris-Onnophris in the Persea Tree — figs. 4, 16

childhood — 57

choachyte — 84

clap stick — 28, 35; figs. 18, 28

coffin — 15, 18, 21–23, 25, 49, 52–53, 59, 90, 111; figs. 7, 9–10, 37, 39, 60–64, 66–67, 70, 72–73, 75, 77

comb — 62, 64

contract (legal) — 86–87, 91–96

crocodile — 50, 79

Crocodilopolis — 12, 96

CT scan — 23–24, 111–12; figs. 10–13, 60–63, 66

Dakhla Oasis — 12, 88; fig. 53

Dakhla Stela — 88, 90; fig. 53

Deir el-Bahri — 12, 97

Deir el-Medina — 12, 46, 48, 56, 90, 100–01, 103

Dendur — 47

Divine Adoratress of Amun — *see God's Wife of Amun*

divorce — 57, 86, 93–95

djed pillar — 22–23, 28, 32, 42, 80

ear spool — 68, 75

ear stela — 71

Edfu — 12, 49

Edict of Theodosius — 49

education — 57, 90

eldest son (title) — 82, 86–87

employment — 42, 45–46, 55, 98, 100–03, 108; fig. 54

Eye of the Sun, Myth of — 36, 39–40

faience — 19, 23–24, 31, 44–45, 62, 65–68, 77–79; figs. 23, 25

Faiyum — 12, 49–50, 61–62, 85, 92, 95–96

Family Archive from Siut — 87

family structure — 55, 57, 72, 82, 85–86, 88, 90, 92, 94, 108; figs. 41, 48

female figurines — 62, 74–75

fertility — 52, 57, 75–76, 79, 85; fig. 51

Festival of the Valley — 32

First Priest — 13, 15–17, 26–27

food production — 98, 101, 108

footprint — 73

gender roles — 82–83, 85, 103

God's Sealer and Embalmer — 92, 96

God's Wife of Amun — 17, 26, 82; figs. 3–5, 15–16

hair — 18, 25, 28, 32, 34, 36, 42–43, 57, 62, 64–65, 68, 75, 78, 85, 108–09, 111; fig. 47

hair pin — 64

hair ring — 68

hair styling tool — 64

harp — 28, 32, 41; figs. 19, 32

Hathor — 25, 29–33, 35–37, 40, 63, 74; figs. 6, 21–22

Hatmehyet — 78

Hawara — 12, 92, 95–96

hedgehog — 61

Heqet — 76, 79–80

Hermopolis Legal Code — 87, 94

Herodotus — 49–50

hes jar — 44–45; fig. 34

heset — 25–26

Horus — 22, 25, 32, 47, 78, 97

houses — 55, 57–60, 71–72, 74–75, 83–86, 88–90, 92–93, 95–99, 103; figs. 41, 43–46

Hu — 35, 64, 66

ibis — 49, 51; fig. 35

inheritance — 46, 84, 86–88, 91–92, 96

Instructions of 'Onchsheshonqy — 56, 90

Instructions of Any — 56, 76, 82, 84–85

Instructions of Ptahhotep — 56

Isis — 22–23, 26, 37–38, 80, 97

jewelry — 19, 24, 27, 50, 52, 55, 62–63, 65–66, 68, 85, 99

jubilee festival — *see Sed Festival*

ka — 32

Kahun — 99

Karanis — 12, 47

Karnak temple — 12, 15–17, 22, 26–28, 32, 43, 59, 82, 87; figs. 1–4, 16–17, 28, 31

khener — 25, 27–29, 42; fig. 19

Khnum — 23, 80, 88, 91

Khonsu — 32, 39, 82; fig. 30

knife, protective — 72, 76–77

Kom el-Wist — 47

Kom Ombo — 12, 47

Kush — 82, 103

Lebanon — 19

legal rights (of women) — 55, 57, 82–88, 91–92, 94, 96, 99

Lepidotonopolis — 39

lily — 36, 64, 72

linen — 21, 23–24, 43, 49–52, 59, 77, 99, 104, 106, 111; figs. 13, 42

literacy — 48, 57–58, 99

lotus — 43, 63–64

Luxor — 12, 15, 25, 28, 32, 37, 41, 43, 64–65, 67–69, 71–75, 77, 80, 82, 97, 104, 107; figs. 18, 28

marriage — 55–57, 85–86, 90, 92–93, 96

marriage contract — 92–94

Medinet Habu — 12, 37, 58, 65, 67–69, 71–75, 79; fig. 15

medjay — 46

menat necklace — 25, 28–32, 37–40, 46, 74; figs. 17, 20, 25–26, 29, 31

Menhit — 37, 39

Mendes — 12, 78

merchant — 58

Mes, inscription of — 88

Meskhenet — 88, 91

metalworking — 19

mirror — 63

Montu — 26, 97

mummification — 21–24, 49–53, 78, 92, 111; fig. 37

music, function in cult — 25–35, 40, 42–43, 46, 63, 90; figs. 18–19, 22, 24

music, lyrics — 32; fig. 54

musical notation — 32

Mut — 26, 39; fig. 31

nbt pr — 57, 84, 86, 90, 97–99

Nekhbet — 77, 80–81

Nubia — 12, 16, 36, 39, 46, 106–07

Nubian domination — 16–17, 82; fig. 2

Nut — 89

Onuris — 39

Opet Festival — 28, 34; figs. 17–19, 28

oracle — 16, 28, 46–49, 80–81, 88, 91; fig. 53

oracular amuletic decree — 80–81

Osiris — 17–18, 23, 26, 28, 45, 97; figs. 5, 8, 16

Osirix software — 111

ostracon — 46, 84, 90

Ostracon Berlin 10627 — 76, 90

Ostracon Deir el-Medina 116 — 103

Ostracon Deir el-Medina 117 — 103

Ostracon Prague 1826 — 104

papyrus — 30–31, 39, 74, 80–81, 92, 94–95; fig. 22

Papyrus Cairo 65739 — 102

Papyrus Carlsberg 34 — 76, 95–96

Papyrus Carlsberg 36 — 76, 95

Papyrus Carlsberg 589 — 32, 76

Papyrus Copenhagen Hawara 1 — 96

Papyrus Ebers (838) — 76

Papyrus Kahun — 76, 104

Papyrus Louvre 3266 — 91

Papyrus Salt 124 — 104

Papyrus Westcar — 80

Papyrus Wilbour — 84

perfume — 62, 69, 78

phyles — 26

Plucking papyrus for Hathor ritual — 32, 74; fig. 22

pottery — 49, 60, 101, 107, 109; fig. 37

pregnancy — 76–79

property, legal rights to — 84–97

Ptah — 32, 71, 92, 94; fig. 54

razor — 62, 65

Re — 22, 32, 36, 72

Re-Horakhty — 18, 43, 47

Report of Wenamon — 19

Restoration Stela of Tutankhamun — 26–27

(*rmt*) *nmh* (free man/woman/citizen) — 84, 90

sꜣ sign — 80

saddle quern — 109

Saqqara — 12, 40, 44, 51–52, 102; fig. 37

Sed Festival — 28, 32; figs. 14, 20, 34

sekhem sistrum — 30, 32

Sekhmet — 37, 39–40, 89

serpent — 22, 37, 49, 53; fig. 39

servant statues — 101, 108–09

Seshat — 58

Seth — 88-89, 91; fig. 53

shemayet — 25-29

shespet dekhen — 26

Singer in the Interior of the Temple — 15, 21, 24-27, 82; figs. 15-16

sistrum — 25-26, 28-33, 36-37, 40, 46, 74; figs. 5, 17, 19-24, 26

sistrum player — 26, 28, 33, 37

situla — 43-44

Sobek — 49-50

spindle — 99, 106

spindle rod — 99, 106

spindle whorl — 99, 106

spinning bowl — 99, 107

status markers — 16, 33, 57, 82-84, 99, 101; fig. 54

strike (labor) — 99

Tanis — 12-13, 15-16, 19, 45

Taweret — 76-79

teeth — 111; figs. 68-69, 71, 75

Tefnut — 37, 39

textile — 24, 86, 98-100, 102, 105-06, 111

Thoth — 44, 49, 51

tiet ("Isis knot") — 22-23

transfer document — 88, 91-92, 95-96

tweezer — 62, 64

Two Brothers, Story of — 83

votive beds — 74; fig. 22

weaver — 55, 99-101, 106; figs. 55-56

weaving — 86, 99-101, 105

wedjat eye — 22

well — 59, 88-89, 91; fig. 53

Wepwawet — 23, 25

Zeus — 38